CUT TO THE CHASE

Scriptwriting for Beginners

JANET VAN EEDEN

Published in 2023 by Hands-On Books
Cape Town, South Africa

www.modjajibooks.co.za

© Janet van Eeden

Janet van Eeden has asserted her right
to be identified as the author of this work.

All rights reserved.

No part of this book may be reproduced or
transmitted in any form or by any means, mechanical
or electronic, including photocopying or recording, or
be stored in any information storage or retrieval system
without permission from the publisher.

Cover artwork by Jesse Breytenbach

Book layout by Andy Thesen

Set in Stone

ISBN: 978-1-928215-91-2

ISBN ebook: ISBN 978-1-991240-06-4

FOREWORD

Janet van Eeden and I met at Rhodes University Drama Department in 1978. Many years later we worked together when I directed two plays that she had written. Theatre, for me, has always been the Engine Room of all Dramatic endeavours: Be it Acting, Writing or Directing. Her grounding as a writer was thus in the tough immediacy of seeing your work performed live in front of an audience. The hard yards. The stone quarry on Robben Island. She has gone on to achieve a doctorate in the game.

In this book she will bring to the reader the benefits of those valuable experiences and lessons learnt by DOING, and not Dreaming of Doing. Google is not your Aunty. Experience is.

Janet's cause is the reason I write like I do. The way she has continued ever forward in her career … no matter what. It inspires me to keep writing too.

All the best to all readers!

Ian Roberts
– veteran actor, director and writer of innumerable films, television productions and theatre plays

CONTENTS

INTRODUCTION	1
CHAPTER ONE What is Scriptwriting?	3
CHAPTER TWO Characters	16
CHAPTER THREE Structure	26
CHAPTER FOUR The Pitch's the Thing …	42
CHAPTER FIVE The Right Treatment …	56
CHAPTER SIX Finding the Beat	89
CHAPTER SEVEN What Defines Writing for Film?	111
CHAPTER EIGHT Crowdfunding What is Crowdfunding?	180
CONCLUSION	189
Feedback	192
References	197

INTRODUCTION

So many people watch films and yet so few know how to write film scripts. Scriptwriting is a very specific art form. Over many years of trying to teach myself to write scripts, I made every mistake you could imagine. Reluctantly, I turned to scriptwriting experts to learn to hone my craft. Using advice from screenwriting experts such as Robert McKee, Linda Seger, Christopher Vogler, among many others, I finally developed a very effective approach to screenwriting. This approach facilitated the production of my first feature script, which was released internationally on the big screen in 2010. It also secured me the services of an agent in London.

The crucial differences between writing for film as opposed to writing for prose will be highlighted and the work of the best film writing gurus will be explored. Scriptwriters will gain insights into the most useful aspects of each specialist's work in a practical way.

This book breaks down the essentials of writing for film. In a series of eight chapters with practical tasks to implement the knowledge given in each section, I unlock the world of scriptwriting for first time scriptwriters, so you don't have to make the same mistakes I did.

Chapter 1

What is Scriptwriting? Introduction to Scriptwriting and the most common storytelling formats, especially the Hero's Journey.

Chapter 2

Characters: Creating believable characters that come to life on screen rather than existing only on the page. Exercises to deepen the world of the character and defining the character's arc or journey will be covered. Examples of successfully constructed films with great character development will be examined.

Chapter 3

Structure: Different ways of structuring a film will be described in more detail, from using a classic three-act structure with a standard Hero's Journey, to exploring multiple-protagonist narratives and other alternative film structures.

Chapter 4

The Pitch: This chapter will encompass the art of writing a good pitch which encapsulates all the essentials of your script. A well-crafted pitch can be used to sell your script. This process ensures that the reader will understands the controlling idea or moral premise behind the story before going any further.

Chapter 5

Treatments: Scriptwriters will be given a step-by-step guide on how to write treatments (an internationally recognised film-selling document) that is used in the film industry worldwide. Without knowing how to write a treatment, a script writer will never sell a story idea.

Chapter 6

Beat Sheets: Scriptwriters will be taught how to write effective beat sheets that evolve into useful **Step Outlines** and that create the basic bones of the script.

Chapter 7

Film Technique: The basics of essential scriptwriting technique, concentrating on format and style as well as the critical and careful use of dialogue, will be explored in this chapter. International conventions will be demonstrated as the standard scriptwriting format and different screenwriting software will be compared. Final Draft is the software I recommend but scriptwriters will be taught to write a script without having to buy any scriptwriting programmes.

Chapter 8

Crowdfunding: What it is, and how can you use it to get your script onto a screen.

Conclusion

There is a step-by-step set of tasks at the end of each chapter so that the scriptwriter can slowly but surely write their own film script.

By the end of this manual, the writer will have been guided towards writing a well-thought-out first draft script – formatted to internationally acceptable scriptwriting standards.

Chapter 1

WHAT IS SCRIPTWRITING?

1. The Back Story – My Own Hero's Journey

The Ordinary World

> *You will never write a good book until you have written some bad ones.* – George Bernard Shaw

I read this apparently simple quote many years ago. It struck me as a good starting point to talk about writing plays, whether they are for stage or for screen. My original motto in play and screenwriting was borrowed from Nike, and I used to just do it. Writing, that is. And I wrote a lot of bad plays in the early days.

The Inciting Incident

I started writing plays and screenplays seriously after the well-known actor Richard E Grant (blessed be REG forever) answered a letter I'd written to him. I'd taken the unusual step of sending a letter to his agent after I'd had a dream (I know …) about a film I'd written in which he was the star. In the dream I felt very strongly that I *had* to become a screenwriter. This was such an unusual thought to me as I'd never ever seen a screenplay before. So I made a deal with myself: I would write to REG and, if he answered my letter, I would attempt to write the script I'd dreamt about. After receiving his kind letter, I had to undertake the terrifying process of attempting to write a screenplay. Having never seen a screenplay before, never mind having written one, my first attempt was a fairly monstrous creation. It was three times longer than it should have been; it was so dialogue-heavy that it would never have made it to the screen, and it was too soppy and personal ever to see the light of day. According to the deal I'd made with myself, I sent it to REG, and yes, I blush still at the recollection of my bravado. But dear REG (blessed be …) criticised it honestly and gave me sharp but sensible advice about how to transform it from a being really good doorstop into becoming perhaps a usable script. His exact words were, in case you're interested: "Cut! Cut! Cut! Screenplays are around 90 pages. Be brutal with it." I shudder to think now that I'd sent him a 300-page monstrosity.

Crossing the Threshold

REG's feedback was enough to keep me going for a number of years. That, as well as a few small nibbles of positive encouragement, such as a script being optioned for production by an actual film production company, stopped me from giving it all up and becoming a mielie farmer in the Free State.

Tests, Trials and Allies

Trying to get a script made into a film is ridiculously difficult. For example, I spent more than five years working on a single project with a British producer (thanks to my agent in London) with a series of insane – it has to be said – directors who made me change the script continually on what seemed like daily whims. For example, one director insisted immediately on changing strong female characters into male characters, turning one well-motivated murder into hundreds of dead bodies scattered over the veld, reducing an intelligent story into a salacious murder romp with a seriously racist twist. Each time he asked for changes, I would rewrite the whole 110 pages of the script from the beginning, all without receiving a single penny in payment. Legally, producers can option a script for $1 and promise the rest of the payment for the writer on first day of principal photography. You have been warned.

Approach to the Innermost Cave

In the end, the producer who'd used my screenplay as the script to apply for funds from the UK Film Council and other funders, dropped my script and used another script from another writer to make her film. I had no recourse to any compensation, and I'm not afraid to say that I had a bit of a melt-down and a crisis of faith after the brutal five-year process.

So, having studied Speech and Drama at Rhodes University and having lived a life so full of drama it wouldn't be believed if put into production, I felt entitled to write a stage play – especially as I'd been frustrated by the lack of autonomy when writing film scripts. Writing for theatre put the power back into my own hands. Sometimes a writer has to become her own producer, however reluctantly, if she wants her work to see the light of day. For the next few years I wrote a play a year and succeeded in raising funds from the National Arts Council, which allowed me to produce the plays professionally and take them on tour.

Even while putting on the plays, I continued to travel the unforgiving road of scriptwriting for many different producers – a few in this country strung me along for a number of years too. Along with the stage plays, I'd write a screenplay a year. While doing so, I became aware of the need to learn a little more about structure. After thinking I never wanted anyone to tell me what or how to write, I listened to my agent and the fickle producers in London and forced myself to read the revered scriptwriting guru of the 90s, **Robert McKee**. His book *Story* became the stick with which producers beat beleaguered scriptwriters. They would quote him verbatim when they weren't sure of what else to say in order to put off making your film for another year or two. As I hate being told how to do anything by anyone, I especially resented being told how to write screenplays by an American (McKee) who'd only had one of his ten film scripts made into an actual film. But I recognised that I had to learn the screenwriting jargon merely to survive in the slick world of international film production.

To my surprise, especially as I hold the creative process sacred, I had to admit that learning a little about story structure taught me a lot more about how to write plays. I took what made sense from McKee and applied it to my own work. As soon as I did this, my plays improved dramatically. Pardon the pun. And screenplay writing didn't feel quite as hit-and-miss as it had before.

However, I still remain firmly averse to the pundits who insist that on page 25 I should have my first turning point and on page 60 the second act plot twist should kick in. (I've actually had a script editor phone me and ask why there isn't a twist on page 25.

I couldn't believe that she'd stuck to a template so literally. That jargon, by the way, is classic Syd Field. He is another of the gods to whom many script editors and producers ritually sacrifice virgin scriptwriters. I did succumb and bought one of his many books, *Screenplay: The Foundations of Screenwriting*. After almost dying of shock at how prescriptive he is, I've promised myself to use the book to extract whatever is useful in it.)

The Reward

Another exceptionally useful guru for scriptwriters came across my radar just after I'd discovered McKee. He is Christopher Vogler. His book, *The Writer's Journey: Mythic Structure for Storytellers*, proved invaluable in finally getting my first (though by no means the first I'd written) screenplay into production. This script was *White Lion*, which was released onto the big screen internationally in 2010. Vogler's work also led me to explore the originator of his theory, Joseph Campbell, whose work, *The Hero with a Thousand Faces*, is a thorough analysis of what commonalities exist in stories across all religions, cultures and races. It just happens to be a useful guide for writing resonant stories. Campbell proposed that human beings share a similar understanding of mythical symbols in our make-up, and his work enhanced the understanding Carl Jung had given us into the understanding of humanity's shared collective unconscious and recognition of archetypes.

The Road Back

When you start exploring the world of screenwriting, before you commit to the arduous journey, you should ask yourself why you want to write drama, whether on screen or on stage, rather than other genres. To choose to write plays one has to have a passion for telling stories in a dramatic way, whether it is on the stage or in film.

Return with the Elixir

One way to find out if you are really suited to this art form is to see whether you enjoy watching people and wondering about their motivations. This, to me, is the absolute joy of writing dramatically, putting people on a stage, giving them lines, and trying to obscure their motivations from the audience for as long as possible. Being obvious in the motivations of one's characters removes the element of surprise for the audience, and is often referred to as being "on the nose" with one's writing. People seldom say exactly what they are thinking or feeling in real life. Imagine how risky it would be to blurt out that:

a) you are passionately in love with someone who is already married;
b) you wish you could kill someone because (s)he is married to the person you are passionately in love with;
c) you are bored to death by the person who is passionately in love with you.

One of my greatest joys is to find dialogue that conveys not only something of the subtext of a character but that takes one inevitably along the path of finding out exactly who that character is. As McKee says, "True character emerges under pressure." So if you like writing about how people react to situations in which they are under pressure, write plays or screenplays. If you like writing deep, introspective reflections about how the character feels when under pressure, write novels. And remember the old maxim of the dramatic medium: **show** (the reactions of characters), don't **tell**. This is even more important when writing screenplays. If a line of dialogue can be cut in favour of a visual scene or action on camera, **cut the line**.

The second question I'm often asked is where do I find ideas for stories? McKee says that a dysfunctional childhood is the perfect qualification for being a great writer. So I'm alright, then. But what if you haven't had a terrible childhood? I try to get my scriptwriters to think about a character first before they find a story.

A simple way to find a character as a starting point is to watch people around you. Try to imagine what sort of daily life the homeless man on the corner, sitting with his ancient, grizzled mother/wife, must have. Or watch the woman struggling with two small toddlers and a wayward shopping trolley who looks as if she could have been a model. What would her life have been like if she hadn't become frazzled by domestic chores? If you are a writer your imagination will kick in very quickly and you'll have a hundred stories after one morning of watching the people around you.

As I said, focusing on a specific character is a great way of finding a story. However, sometimes stories find you. Personally, my dreams are a great source of inspiration, and some of my most off-the-wall stories have come from dreams which have woken me with their absurdity.

If you are completely stuck, though, read through a newsfeed, online or in print, and examine any one of the stories that grab your attention. Think of the story behind the characters in the story.

Sometimes, you will just have something you want to say about a certain issue. I advise you very strongly then just to get on and say it.

As for developing a germ of a storyline into a screenplay, I've become a great believer in teaching the basics of the classic three-act structure until writers are adept enough to break the rules. At its most basic, writers should understand the Aristotelian three-act structure and create a story with a beginning, a middle and an end. Act 1 should be the set-up of the story, Act 2 the development and complication of the set-up and should be the longest section of the screenplay and Act 3 is the pay-off, where all the loose ends are tied up and satisfaction is given to the audience, one hopes.

Once you have mastered this simple structure, without falling into deeply prescriptive territory, you can break rules with impunity. One of my brightest screenwriters once wrote a screenplay that broke all the rules and became a parody of storytelling and the hero's journey itself. It was a very good screenplay, but he had to know the rules before he could write well enough to break them.

If you need even more assistance in finding your path in a story, I recommend Chris Vogler's *The Writer's Journey*, which need not become prescriptive but can really help you plot your path if you are lost. In fact, George Lucas attributes his success with the first *Star Wars* to discovering Joseph Campbell's *The Hero with a Thousand Faces* when he was completely at a loss in his script. Chris Vogler based his book on Joseph Campbell's work, which he said "unlocked the secret code of storytelling". Both are well worth reading.

Character revealed through dialogue

Characterisation is one of the most challenging issues. If characters are to be more than one-dimensional I can't help thinking one needs to know quite a bit about the world and be a good observer of people. As

I said earlier, people seldom say exactly what they think, so learning to be oblique in your dialogue is a really good way to cultivate your screenwriting craft.

Another helpful thing to remember is that the most interesting characters usually have contradictory elements to them. Think of a conservative Bohemian; an obsessive/compulsive psychologist; an ambitious hippie ... you could go on all day. McKee refers to Hamlet as one of the world's most multi-dimensional characters, and I agree. At times Hamlet is deeply depressed or he is manically happy. Sometimes he is wise. At other times he is rash. He is loving and gentle one moment, then harsh and reproachful another. But yes, he is an extreme character and perhaps he would be diagnosed with bipolar disorder these days. Somewhere along that continuum of Hamlet's extreme behaviour is the need to create a character who is not a one-dimensional stereotype. McKee also says that making Hamlet interact with different characters who bring out different aspects of his erratic personality is the secret of the play's success. This is one of Bob's cleverer moments and leads me perfectly to the next point. Hamlet's interaction with the variety of characters he encounters showcases his change in character through the varied dialogue he uses with each one.

Dialogue is vital in a screenplay if you are to show many facets of a character. I always say to my writers that the minute they start to hear a character's voice in their heads, they are ready to start writing the screenplay. I usually get writers to write monologues for their main characters as a way to make their characters come to life and to give them voice.

One has to be very restrained about dialogue, though. As someone who just loves dialogue, I have been known to over-write speeches, especially when I first started writing screenplays. Remember REG and the 300-page script I sent him? But once you have found your character's voice, try to think of ways that the audience can learn more about that character when (s)he is talking to different characters. Think of Hamlet talking to Polonius as opposed to his talking to Ophelia. How different is he when he is talking to his best friend, Horatio? Compare his speech with Horatio after he has just talked to his despised stepfather, Claudius.

Once again, listen to people around you and observe the nuances of speech they use in real life. There is no better teacher.

2. Essential Tools: The Hero's Journey – The Nuts and Bolts of Storytelling

Good storytellers have always known one thing: people love to hear a story about an underdog who has to overcome huge obstacles against the odds, an underdog who has every evil twist of fate thrown at him to thwart his success, an underdog who looks like they might not actually make it to the end. And of course, every good story ensures that this poor, brow-beaten underdog is made of enough indomitable spirit to overcome all the odds. Usually, in spite of it all, our beloved underdog succeeds.

Oral storytellers relied on this formula for success; ancient mythologies used this recipe and even very good sport promoters use this outline. How many of us have cheered for the team that isn't the favourite? For the player who has had the most injuries? Just think of South Africa and the 1995 Rugby World Cup. Think of the South African cricket team at the Cricket World Cup and Bafana Bafana. They have been the underdogs for far too long, and yet we keep hoping that one day they will succeed.

The point is that all good stories – the ones that keep you emotionally invested right until the end – usually have a hero or heroine we are rooting for. We love these heroes in spite of their flaws, and we are with them every step of the way as they go through enormous battles to complete their journeys of self-discovery.

Many religions and mythologies follow the pattern of a deity's struggle too. Just think of how abused, mocked and maligned Jesus was. But the story of his resurrection was a victory over the odds in the most supernatural way.

Three Common Archetypes

In the early twentieth century Carl Jung, a student of Sigmund Freud's, broke away from Freud's sexual obsessions and devised his own belief system based largely on the idea that humanity shared a set of symbols that are universally recognised. Jung studied dreams, mythologies, religions and different cultures and discovered that humankind shared a common set of stock characters. He believed that there were standard recognisable characters, which kept cropping up in stories and myths throughout the world and which played universally recognisable symbolic roles. He called these archetypes. One example of an archetype is the Wise Old Man, a recurring figure in so many fairy tales and stories. Think of Merlin, Gandalf the Grey, Dumbledore the Wizard, tribal elders and sangomas. There are also the Wise Old Women: the witches with supernatural insights in *Macbeth*, ancient female crones in fairy tales, and again, the mythic import of female sangomas. Both the Wise Old Man and the Wise Old Woman help young heroes find their way on their personal journeys. Other archetypes are the young ingénue, the Innocent Virgin or the anima as Jung called her (Cinderella, Little Red Riding and Snow White). There are many more lesser known ones, such as the Threshold Guardian, the Shapeshifter and the Shadow. But for our storytelling purposes here the most important archetype is **the Hero**. I'm not differentiating between hero and heroine as I believe the hero is both masculine and feminine.

The **Hero,** who often has a flaw, has to overcome many, many odds. They fight all the battles we wish we were strong enough to fight ourselves. They are one of our most powerful archetypes. For storytelling purposes the role of the hero is crucial because of **audience identification**. Think of Hercules, Ulysses, Moses, Hamlet, Indiana Jones, Joan of Arc and more recently, James Bond, Shrek, Katniss Everdeen, Hermione Granger, and many more.

Classic Structure

Picking up where Jung left off, a writer and academic named **Joseph Campbell** began to analyse the similarities between myths, legends and archetypes. He spent much of his life devoted to comparing common themes in world mythologies and great stories. Eventually he wrote a book that changed the way people viewed storytelling. It was called *The Hero With a Thousand Faces*. In this he showed that there is a classic structure behind most, if not all, of the best stories in the world. He clarified this structure and wrote a blueprint that could be applied to most stories.

In the 1970s a struggling first-time writer/director discovered *The Hero with a Thousand Faces*. He had been stuck in development hell for years with his story about a fictional, futuristic world in which a young man called Luke had to find his way. Desperate for help, he applied Joseph Campbell's structure to his unwieldy story and, just like magic, found his way into a classic hero's journey. The young writer/director was George Lucas, and his story was a little tale called *Star Wars*.

In 1992, **Christopher Vogler** adapted Joseph Campbell's *The Hero With a Thousand Faces* into a simpler structure, specifically for use in films. As Vogler says, "Campbell had broken the secret code of story, with its set of principles which govern the art of storytelling." As a story analyst for Walt Disney, Vogler wrote a seven-page memo as a practical guide to writing story. Soon this memo became required reading for Disney development executives. It led him to write *The Writer's Journey: Mythic Structure for Storytellers and Screenwriters*.

As Chris Vogler says, "at heart, despite its infinite variety, the hero's story is always a journey (and a transformation). A hero leaves her comfortable, ordinary surroundings to venture into a challenging, unfamiliar world. It may be an outward journey to an actual place ... but there are many journeys which take the hero on an inward journey, one of the mind, the heart, the spirit. In any good story the hero grows and changes, making a journey from one way of being to the next: from despair to hope, weakness to strength, folly to wisdom, love to hate, and back again. It's these emotional journeys that hook an audience and make a story worth watching."

In the process of overcoming many challenges, the hero must go through a transformation, attaining things that they set out to get or that were lacking in the beginning. We can identify "outer missions", which are tangible goals that need to be accomplished, like destroying the death star in *Star Wars*. We can also identify "inner missions", which are more personal and introspective for a hero, like Luke needing to become an adventuring Jedi knight.

The Hero's Journey Breakdown

Chris Vogler's **Hero's Journey** is equated opposite with scriptwriting terms from Aristotle, Dr Linda Seger, Robert McKee, Joseph Campbell and Syd Field on the right.

In summation, the hero's journey ensures that your character goes on a journey from the beginning of the film to the end, and emerges at the end of the film as different person with new insights. This journey of enlightenment is known as the **character's arc**. Your hero may still find themselves in the same situation as they were before but they should be enriched with insights and wisdom from the journey

THE HERO'S JOURNEY

ACT 1

(BEGINNING – Aristotle)

Ordinary World – Vogler, Campbell (*Set Up* – Dr Linda Seger)

Call to Adventure – Vogler, Campbell (*Inciting incident* – McKee, *Catalyst* – Dr Linda Seger)

Refusal of the Call – Vogler, Campbell

Meeting the Mentor – Vogler (*Wise Old Man/Wise Old Woman* – Campbell)

Crossing the (First) Threshold – Vogler, Campbell (20–30 pages – Field, *1st Act Turning Point* – Dr Linda Seger)

ACT 2

DEVELOPMENT – Seger

(*MIDDLE* – Aristotle)/

Tests, Allies, Enemies – Vogler, Campbell (*Obstacle* – Dr Linda Seger)

Approach to Innermost Cave – Vogler (*Complication* – Dr Linda Seger, *Approach to Darkest Moment* – Campbell)

(**Midpoint** – McKee, Field, *Point of No Return* – Dr Linda Seger)

Ordeal – (*CRISIS* – Aristotle, *Darkest Moment* – Campbell, *Reversal* – Dr Linda Seger)

Reward – Vogler (*Seizing the Sword* – Campbell, 50–60 pages – Field, *CATHARSIS* – Aristotle, *2nd Act Turning Point* – Dr Linda Seger)

ACT 3

RESOLUTION – Dr Linda Seger

(*END* – Aristotle)

The Road Back – Vogler, Campbell

Resurrection – Vogler, Campbell (*CLIMAX* – Aristotle, *Denouement* – McKee, *Climax* – Dr Linda Seger)

Return With the Elixir – Vogler, Campbell (20–30 pages – Field)

(Van Eeden, 2019)

they've been on. In a tragedy, the hero doesn't come out alive, but should still die with enlightenment, or have passed on the wisdom from their life to another character.

1. Watch a few classic hero's journeys and see if you can mark the various turning points, a phrase used by McKee to mark each one of the stages on the hero's journey. Some of the best to watch for a step-by-step breakdown of Vogler's journey are:

   Star Wars (1977)
   Rocky (1976)
   The Shawshank Redemption (1994)
   The Lion King (1994)
   Braveheart (1995)
   The Matrix (1999)
   Gladiator (2000)
   Erin Brockovich (2000)
   The Lord of the Rings (2001–2003)
   The Pursuit of Happyness (2006)
   Jerusalema (2008)
   Invictus (2009)
   Mandela: Long Walk to Freedom (2013)
   Hard to Get (2014)
   Bohemian Rhapsody (2018)
   Joker (2019)

2. Add your own favourites to your list.

TASKS

1. Write a monologue for your central character, writing their thoughts in a stream of consciousness flow. What to look for here is a unique voice that makes your character interesting. Why would an audience want to hear what they have to say? What makes their life experience more interesting than the average? Your character must have insights or life experiences which sets them apart from others. Just try to listen for your character's voice and write down what they say. Try not to censor yourself at this stage. Just let your character's voice flow.

2. Using the character you have discovered in your monologue, try to chart a sequence of events using Chris Vogler's hero's journey as a guide. You do not need to stick to this accurately but use the larger outline as a blueprint to make sure your character goes on a journey that changes them. The **inciting incident** or **call to adventure** is one of the most important aspects of finding the journey of your character at this point. What is going to propel your character onto a new path – leaving the ordinary world of their comfort zone for the new world of adventure and self-discovery? Something big has to happen to make the journey begin.

3. Chart the progress of your character in a short sequence of events alongside the hero's journey. I attach a breakdown of the deconstruction of *White Lion's* journey (page 98). Yours does not have to be as detailed but you will get an idea of what I want you to do in this section. This is the most difficult part of the writing of your script, and it will take a number of revisions to have an outline that you will be able to use as the foundation for your script. Your first attempt will not necessarily be the right one, but I will guide you towards making the beat sheet work for you in Chapter 6.

READING LIST

Field, Syd. *The Screenwriter's Workbook*. Dell, 1984.
McKee, Robert. *Story: Substance, Structure, Style and the Principles of Screenwriting*. Methuen, 1998.
Seger, Linda. *Making a Good Script Great*. Samuel French, 2010.
Vogler, Christopher. *Writer's Journey: Mythic Structure for Storytellers and Screenwriters*. Boxtree, 1996.

Chapter 2

CHARACTERS

1. Who's Who? The Big Picture

What is character? It's a term bandied about freely, but what does the word really mean? *Chambers Concise 20th Century Dictionary* says that character pertaining to a human being is "the aggregate of peculiar qualities which constitutes personal or national individuality: especially moral qualities".

Moral Qualities

I think this is a good place to start when dealing with character. Chambers' description talks about moral qualities. This definition leads me straight into one of the strongest proponents of the morality of characters: Lajos Egri.

Egri, in his many books on scriptwriting, talks about the "moral premise" of the main character as being the backbone of the story. I must admit to being baffled when I first came across this term. I didn't know exactly what he meant by this, especially as I'd written stories from the point of view of simply following a story's natural progression for many years. I'd never even considered the moral journey of my characters in such a definite way.

After wrestling with a number of stories I'd already written by the time I came across Egri's moral premise theory, I realised that some of the problems in my scripts were often compounded because I had not been particularly clear about the elusive moral premise of the central characters while writing.

In Other Words

To try and explain this more clearly: the moral premise is the equivalent of what Robert McKee calls the **controlling idea**. This controlling idea should guide and shape the ultimate message that you want the audience to take from your story. This idea should come across in everything the character says and does and everything the audience sees on the screen. Therefore, every writing choice should be determined by the controlling idea.

If this sounds complicated, it isn't really. The controlling idea is something you employ instinctively, to some extent, when writing. But, for the purposes of crafting your writing, you have to make yourself much more aware of it. In this way you can make conscious story choices to ensure that the controlling idea remains clear and un-muddied. Writing with conscious awareness of the moral premise removes the dangers of a hit-and-miss approach.

I've discovered that the reason some of the plays, film scripts and stories I'd written didn't appeal to most was because I hadn't been as clear as I'd thought about the character's moral premise. So, even though *I* knew what I meant about the character's journey, others didn't, as I hadn't made the character's internal motivations concrete enough to come across on the stage, page or screen.

Character's internal conflict/Moral premise

Think very carefully about what it is that you want people to take away from your story. Usually the meaning you want to convey plays out through the central **conflict** of the character, both their external and internal conflicts.

For example, in the film *Braveheart*, William Wallace's character is fighting an unjust system: the English nobility's brutal reign over the Scots. This is his external journey. His internal journey is to overcome his own sense of inferiority or lack of self-worth in the face of the oppression of the Scots.

William Wallace's moral journey is to fight for Scotland (external journey) and to fight for his own personal freedom (internal journey) even if it costs him his life. Every frame of the film works towards this end. Finally, the message viewers take away from the story is this: personal freedom and integrity are worth more than life itself. This is the moral premise of *Braveheart*.

A few more examples of the moral premise of a number of well-known films:
- *Silence of the Lambs*: Courage destroys evil.
- *Titanic*: Love conquers death.

- *American Beauty*: Integrity overcomes superficiality, or truth outweighs appearances.
- *Little Miss Sunshine*: Honesty beats superficiality, or winning is not about coming first.

The last two films show how differently very similar moral premises can be explored. Although *American Beauty* and *Little Miss Sunshine* both explore the way integrity is compromised in the superficial aspects of American society, they do so in completely different ways.

To put it another way, the moral premise examines the values of the characters involved in the story – which gives the world in which these values will be explored its deeper meaning.

To put the idea of the moral premise in the simplest way possible: it is all about positive and negative values (good/bad, weak/strong, honest/dishonest, integrity/deception, deluded/enlightened and so on) and the journey your character takes to get to either of these extremes or to somewhere in between.

I will come back to the idea of the moral premise after you have completed a few exercises to help you define your character's journey.

2. The Details – Clarifying Character

To bring the search for character back to a few practical exercises before getting lost in the search for a moral premise, let's start with the basics.

You should have written a monologue and a **beat sheet** by now and should have a fairly good idea of the external shape of the story you want to tell. In essence you should have the spine of your plot more or less constructed in a way that appeals to you, and your character should be comfortably ensconced in your plot line.

It's essential at this stage to still be drawn to your character. By this I mean that you still feel keen to write about them. If you are bored with your character at this point, you need to drop this particular story at once and find a new one. If your character or story bores you after a few days or even weeks of working on it, it can never hope to entertain an audience.

If this unfortunate incident has happened, it would be best to search for a new character "with legs", as I call it. This means that your character should be complex enough to intrigue you for a long time, sometimes for even years of rewrites. (This is not an exaggeration. There are many scripts I've worked on for close to 20 years and I'm still not bored of them.)

Your character will have legs if they have enough complexity to give you lots of room for character development. For example, writing a story about a nun who has given her life to God and who has been in a convent for 17 years and who has no doubts about her vocation is not particularly rich material for development. However, if that same nun suddenly receives a letter from a child she'd given up for adoption when she was 16, before she went into the convent, then we have a story on our hands. If that child is a daughter asking her mother to help her now that she, too, is pregnant and alone, we heighten the conflict even more.

Why is this kind of complexity good for character? Well, as I said above, your character needs to have room to develop. In the nun story above, we realise that this apparently pious nun isn't quite as innocent as she likes to portray. She has a flawed past which makes her all the more intriguing.

Why do we like a flawed character? Because then we are assured that there will be conflict in our story. An internal conflict is essential at least, because our character needs to have a moral dilemma to add drama. As you know by now, all good stories are about **conflict**. Without conflict there is no story. Ideally, we would want our character to have both **internal** and **external** conflict.

In our nun's case, her internal conflict would be whether to deny her daughter's existence or to help and support her child after all these years, especially as she has experienced the same crisis herself. Her external conflict is whether to be honest to the rest of the convent about her conflicted past, or whether to renounce her vows to take her place in the world with her daughter.

Another way to put it is to say that the internal conflict is an invisible, inner conflict and the external conflict is visible in the character's external circumstances.

Discussing moral dilemma brings us right back into the territory of Lajos Egri's moral premise.

So, to reiterate, we need a character to have a discrepancy or flaw to make them interesting and to give our story somewhere to go: i.e., "legs". This is how you're going to ensure that your character is more than one dimensional and will captivate an audience.

TASKS

a. Explore your character's inner contradictions in one or two sentences

Examine the conflict in your character's make-up. Define something in your character that is a contradiction. For example, is your character a fitness fanatic whose secret flaw is that he is really phobic about becoming the fat boy he once was at school?

Or is she an aging hippie who dreams of free love and peace but who is so deeply conventional in her soul that she won't allow her 17-year-old daughter to go out on a date with a boy?

Here are a few more quick examples:
- A woman dying for recognition from the art world but too crippled by shyness to exhibit her paintings;
- An altruistic nurse who cares for neglected orphans but who ignores her aged mother's very simple needs;
- A world leader who can't control his wife's wild sexual behaviour.

You get the idea. Remember, you are not looking for characters as one-dimensional as Superman but you want their dilemmas to live on in the minds of your audiences forever. If possible, of course.

One classic complex character is Humphrey Bogart's Rick in *Casablanca*. This character's unusual behaviour is one of the reasons why this film has lived on in people's imaginations. Rick is the ultimate self-serving mercenary, right until the moment he commits an unprecedented act of self-sacrifice for the woman he loves.

Clarify exactly what it is your character wants. If you are able to at this point, try to separate their internal desire from their external desire.

Your main character, the **protagonist** of your story, must **want** something. Taking into account that in all compelling dramas the protagonist has a deep **desire** for something, define what this one thing is that your character wants.

This desire is what drives the **plot/action** along. Without your character desiring something outside of his or her normal state of being (or ordinary world) we do not have a journey. Therefore, it is important to ensure that the object your character desires is deeply compelling. The more compelling it is, the more the **STAKES** will be raised for your character if he or she loses this one thing. The higher the stakes, the more riveting the drama, and the more compelled we'll be to watch.

b. Who or what is your antagonist? Make them as threatening as possible

The next thing to ask is **who** does your protagonist want this elusive something from? Is this person apparently in the way of your character achieving their desire strong enough to be the **antagonist**? That is, is the character blocking your character from achieving their aim in the story a worthy opponent?

Have a quick think back to the old cowboy films. The more compelling the baddies in the black hats were, the more we admired the heroes in the white hats.

The strength of your antagonist is vital. Even if your antagonist is an idea or an ideology such as the state, communism, the army, the enemy at war and so on, the perceived threat for your character has to be real so that we can engage with the difficulty of our hero's journey.

Just have a quick think of your favourite screen characters for a moment. I'm willing to bet that quite a few of them are the baddies. Who can forget Anthony Hopkins' iconic performance as Hannibal Lecter? Clarice would have been so much less of an intriguing character if her antagonist in *The Silence of the Lambs* had been any less evil.

Have you heard the phrase "up the ante"? It means you have to increase the threat. This can take be done by increasing the power the antagonist holds over your character thereby increasing their chances of losing what they desire. This will increase the dynamic compulsion of your story. This is worth bearing in mind as you work on this exercise.

1. What would happen to your character if they achieved their heart's desire?
2. What would happen if they didn't achieve their heart's desire?
3. What does your character want? And what do you think they need instead?

Bearing in mind the answers you've given, think seriously about what your character **thinks** they **want**.

This is a very serious issue. Almost always, what a character **wants** is not always what he **needs**. There's a wonderful song by *The Rolling Stones* with words along the same lines. This song was played regularly as a theme song in the brilliant US TV series, *House*. The character House never gets what he wants but he usually gets what he needs.

This is true for your character too. What she *thinks* she wants is usually not what she *needs* for moral growth and for enlightenment. Think about this for a moment and see if you can define these two vital differences for your character.

4. For a deeper understanding of your character, in the light of the above decisions you've made, think about the following:
    - What is your character's favourite item of clothing?
    - What is their pet hate?
    - What are they afraid of?
    - What would make them laugh?
    - What would make them cry?
    - What are they ashamed of – something in their past, for example?

c. Write down the characters

Do your answers to the questions above make you change any external aspects of your character or their antagonist? If so, how?

At this stage, I am assuming that you know the age, sex, look of your character.

Write all of these statements down and keep them in a file called Character Work for each character. Refer to this file throughout the writing process and make additions whenever necessary.

d. Now for a bit of fun homework

Choose a film that you love. If you don't have a particular favourite, you can use one of mine. *Little Miss Sunshine* is such a delightful film that I refer to it often as a marvel of character creation as well as great scriptwriting. The scriptwriter and director have created a unity of character and visual scenes that seems quite effortless but is very well crafted.

Whether you use *Little Miss Sunshine* or another film, watch the opening few minutes with great attention.

In *Little Miss Sunshine*, the characters are defined from the second they first appear in the frame.

The opening sequence is classic. Olive played by Abigail Breslin is defined in a few exceptionally well-chosen shots. First, we see a close-up shot of her eyes, wearing large unattractive glasses. The glasses are reflecting a beauty pageant beaming from the television screen she's watching. That single shot sums up little Olive's desire, her aspirations and her journey through the film. She wants to be a beauty pageant queen.

A longer shot of her a few seconds later shows us that she is a plump little girl, her large tummy making her an unlikely candidate for beauty pageant queen or even a princess. In that second shot we see her "flaw" in terms of the story. She's not beauty pageant fodder. But here comes our internal conflict: in her heart Olive believes she is a beauty queen and it's the only thing she really wants.

Her external conflict comes from her trying to get to a beauty pageant in time when it is far away from her home.

In case you are watching the film for the first time I won't say any more, but I will point out how right it is that she doesn't get what she wants, but she gets what she needs instead. And how right that feels by the end of this charming film.

Refer to *Little Miss Sunshine's* moral premise up above and see if this still rings true for you.

The rest of the opening sequence, which is brilliantly done to coincide with the title credit of *Little Miss Sunshine*, depicts each of the subsequent characters with equally effective strokes. See if you can define their characters and their flaws for yourself by watching this opening sequence.

The first words of the father, Richard, are very telling. What does he say that gives us clues into his psyche? How does his dress sense play into his character?

The teenage step-son is seen bench-pressing weights. There's a poster of the philosopher Nietzsche on his bedroom wall. He crosses off his exercise routine determinedly on a hand-drawn schedule. What does each action and object in his room say about him? Observe how his T-shirts make comments throughout the film even though he has taken a vow of silence.

Observe the details with Grandpa, the mother and then her brother. Each frame tells us an enormous amount about each character, whether they use dialogue or not.

It is interesting to note that this film does not have one single main character or protagonist. It is a multiple protagonist film in which each of the characters goes on their own journey or **character arc**.

Also consider the role of the Volkswagen Kombi in this film. How important is this vehicle in terms of the film? Is it a metaphor for anything? If so, what?

e. Choose a film to watch

If you can't watch *Little Miss Sunshine*, choose another film and see whether the opening scenes of the film define the character's inner and outer conflicts or journeys as clearly as the one I've used as an example.

Think about ways you could convey your character's inner and outer journey in a visual way on screen.

Can you think of any objects in the film you watched that become metaphors?

f. Character arcs

What is your character's moral journey? What is their inner conflict or the flaw they have to overcome? How is this reflected in their external conflict or in their environment? Put this into a simple statement that will become your controlling idea for every word you write for every frame of your film.

The term **character arc** refers to the development of the main character as they go on their journey. This arc will be defined by your choice of moral premise.

To give a simpler example, every character that captivates us undergoes a transformation of sorts in a film and overcomes some limitation within themselves. The journey of transformation is known as the **character arc**. Whether your protagonist is a lion, as in *The Lion King*, or a robot as in *WALL-E*, we connect with the characters because of their lessons learnt, which we can relate to in some way, as humans.

The classic *Wizard of Oz* depicts vividly how each character overcomes their inner flaw. The Scarecrow lacks self-belief, the Lion lacks courage, the Tin Man lacks empathy, and Dorothy needs to learn inner peace. Through the course of their journey to Oz, each one of them finds what they are looking for. Each character has moved through a transformation, and we can track their **character arc** from the beginning to the end of their journey.

Recommended reading list

Egri, Lajos. *The Art of Dramatic Writing.* Various Publishers, 1946.

Field, Syd. *The Screenwriter's Workbook.* Dell, 1984.

McKee, Robert. *Story: Substance, Structure, Style and the principles of Screenwriting.* Methuen, 1998.

Seger, Linda. *Making a Good Script Great.* Samuel French, 2010.

Vogler, Chris. *Writer's Journey: Mythic Structure for Storytellers and Screenwriters.* Boxtree, 1996.

Chapter 3

STRUCTURE

Structure is vital

> *Originality is the confluence of content and form: distinctive choices of subject plus a unique shaping of the telling.* – Robert McKee

1. Structure is Storytelling

As Robert McKee says in his defining work on writing for film, *Story: Substance, Structure, Style and the Principles of Screenwriting*, **content** (which consists of the setting, characters, story ideas and so on) and **form** (which is the selection and arrangement of events, i.e. structure) are inseparable from each other.

He continues the quote above with the words: "With content in one hand and a mastery of form in the other, a writer **sculpts** story". I love the image of a writer as a sculptor. Knowing how to use structure well gives the writer the tools in which they can create a thing of beauty, a work that is out of the ordinary and something that will be remembered for years to come.

Now that you have found out **what** you want to write about in your film through doing the exercises in Chapter 1 and Chapter 2, the next most important question is **how** will you tell that story? Once again, your choice of **how** you want to tell your particular story makes all the difference. As McKee says:

> *The storyteller's selection and arrangement of events is his master metaphor for the interconnectedness of all levels of reality – personal, political, environmental and spiritual. Stripped of its surface of characterisation and location, story structure reveals his personal cosmology, his insight into the deepest patterns and motivations for how and why things happen in this world, his view of life's hidden order.*

Jean Anouilh, a 20th-century French dramatist, said: "Fiction gives life its form." As a scriptwriter it is your job to create the shape of the world your characters are going to inhabit to convey an insight into your view of the world. Out of the chaos of random events, storytellers have the unique gift of putting events in a specific order to create something with deeper meaning for an audience. Your choice of how you shape your particular story will have a huge impact on how the audience will receive it.

Just think of a film such as *Pulp Fiction*. The film created a stir not merely because of its anarchic content of heartless drug dealers and addicts. It created a stir mostly by virtue of its unique form. It was one of the first films to jumble up the standard linear storytelling pattern in a disjointed way. In the randomness of its narrative Quentin Tarantino echoed the chaotic lives of the dissolute people he portrayed. In this particular film, the medium (how the film was portrayed) was part of the message (what it was about).

One thing that is important to note here: while Tarantino apparently shows scant regard for classic storytelling structure in this film, I can tell you without doubt that each one of the seemingly random storylines was plotted in a classic linear narrative before filming. And each one of those characters experiences a standard hero's journey. The ingenuity in *Pulp Fiction* is that the various stories are interwoven randomly and shown out of sequence. The randomness of the form is a very specific choice after very detailed work was done on the classical structure of the storyline. This is true of films such as *Memento, 21 Grams, Babel* and even *Crash*, with its multiple protagonists.

However, as I said earlier, before you are able to start experimenting with different storytelling styles, you have to ensure you know as much as possible about classic storytelling structure. As you can see from the above examples, even experimental structures require you to know the rules before you can break them.

2. Start at the Beginning

You might think we have covered structure already in Chapter 1 with the hero's journey, but we have only just started. The main purpose of teaching the hero's journey in Chapter 1 was to ensure that you create a character who goes on a journey which compels an audience to watch your story. The best way to do this is with the

call to adventure or **inciting incident**, which kicks off all good stories. Once you've chosen a strong event to impel your character on their journey, you have a dramatic question that will **hook** your audience – something that will compel the audience to care about your hero on their journey. That was one of the main reasons I focused on the hero's journey in Chapter 1. A story without a hook is like a sword without a blade: pointless.

The best place to start in our quest to examine structure is to refer to the first person to analyse how drama works: Aristotle. He lived from 384 to 322 BC. His definitive work *Poetics* defined the elements of good drama. Greek theatre was at its height at the time of his writing. The ancient Greeks loved plays about the lives of their kings and gods. From tragedies such as *Oedipus Rex* by Sophocles to silly comedies such as *The Frogs* by Aristophanes, theatre was a cornerstone of Greek life.

Aristotle focused mainly on tragedy and defined certain core tenets of drama. Among them he came up with the following terms:

Mimesis or imitation, representation

Catharsis or, variously, purgation, purification, clarification

Peripeteia or reversal

Anagnorisis or recognition, identification

Hamartia or miscalculation (understood in Romanticism as the tragic flaw)

Mythos or plot

Ethos or character

Dianoia or thought, theme

Lexis or diction, speech

Source: http://en.wikipedia.org/wiki/Poetics_(Aristotle)#Core_terms

It amazes me how Aristotle could define the essentials of drama so specifically all those centuries ago. Today scriptwriting gurus still use terms such as identification, catharsis, reversal, tragic flaw, theme, character, catharsis and plot.

Aristotle also defined the basic structure of a play. He stated that a play should always have a beginning, a middle and an end. This seems so obvious to us nowadays but at that time no one had spelled out the basics of drama structure so clearly before. He also believed that a play should have a unity of time and space, in that events should occur in the fictional world as if they were taking place in a believable world in linear time.

We have progressed too far from Aristotle's first theories. A glut of books about writing for film has flooded the bookshelves in the past few decades. Most of the authors have invented new terms for essentially the same elements of drama that Aristotle defined.

To be fair, writing for film has become a specific art form in itself. However, I must say that I do get tired of the many, many scriptwriting theorists who try to reinvent the wheel.

Below, I'll give you the essential need-to-know information that should guide you towards making the right choice about how to structure your play. Considering that there almost as many books written about scriptwriting as there are scripts written, I'll mention only those which I find invaluable to me.

I've already mentioned Lajos Egri for his work on character, especially. But one of the unassailable and most respected experts in structuring feature film is Syd Field. His books, especially *Screenplay: The Foundations of Screenwriting*, are used as a bible in Hollywood. Even though I don't love his very prescriptive theories, he has described a useful guide for a three-act structure in this way:

Act 1: The Set-up (of the location and characters)

Act 2: The Confrontation (with an obstacle)

Act 3: The Resolution (culminating in a climax and a dénouement)

If you remember the blueprint I drew up of the hero's journey in Chapter 1, you will see Syd Field's terms alongside those of Seger, McKee and Vogler.

While he covers common ground with writers such as McKee and Vogler, Field is more prescriptive than they are about the exact moments (including page numbers!) when certain story events should occur in a script. I'll describe this below and I advise you to use them as a guide only. They're very useful to refer to if you are struggling with your structure.

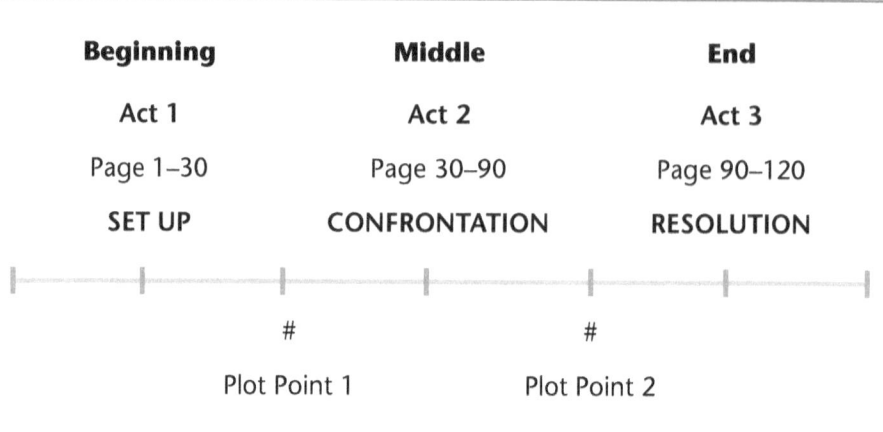

Personally, I never go by his exact page references as I find them a little too prescriptive, but they can be useful as a guide, especially for first time scriptwriters. What is really useful however is to note that his **plot points 1** and **2** come at the end of Acts 1 and 2. Dr Linda Seger was the first theorist to describe these plot points as **turning points**.

Another way to describe the **plot points** or **turning points** is to say that you should have a **twist** at the end of each act. Each of these **twists** should lead logically (but definitely not predictably) to the final **resolution** or **dénouement** of the screenplay. The **dénouement** is the coming together of all the story elements, the tying up of the loose strands, and the moment the audience feels a satisfied "Ah, so that's how it all works out".

These **twists** or **turning points** at the end of each act keep the viewers guessing about the final outcome of the story. Your task is to keep them engaged in your hero's journey. Keeping them guessing ensures that they are **hooked** throughout the film and will watch it to the end.

So to recap, according to Aristotle, Seger, Field, Vogler and McKee, the first act has to **set up** or **establish** the **protagonist** and the **ordinary world** in which they live. In this act, something should happen (an **inciting incident**) to shake the hero out of their comfort zone and create a conflict in their day-to-day world. Without conflict, as you know by now, there is no drama.

This **inciting incident** propels the hero onto a path or journey with consequences. The **inciting incident** or **call to adventure** can take place on- or off-screen. It can also take place in the past and be shown through flashbacks. You can be as creative as you like in structuring exactly where the inciting incident should take place in the narrative. The inciting incident should by its nature raise a **dramatic question** such as "What will happen if …?"

It is vital to phrase your **dramatic question** well in terms of storytelling as how you execute this event will make your film more or less compelling. For example, in *Casablanca*, Rick Blaine (Humphrey Bogart) seems to be quite content with his life as a man making sure his own selfish interests are served during the Second World War. He does business with whoever will serve him best on both sides of the enemy lines. This continues until the arrival of someone from his past. When Ilsa Lund (Ingrid Bergman) arrives, immediately we ask the question: "What if Rick wants to get together with Ilsa again?" and "What is Rick going to do about her husband, who is wanted by the Nazis?" These are great dramatic questions and create an excellent hook into a compelling story which ends in the way we least expect.

In *Braveheart* William Wallace (Mel Gibson) comes back to his native Scotland after living abroad. He is determined to live peacefully in spite of the cruel rule of Edward I who has killed his father and brother. He manages to maintain an apparently peaceful life until his wife, Murron (Catherine McCormack), has her throat slit by the English sheriff. The initial dramatic question asked when the film starts is: Can William Wallace avenge the deaths of his brother and father? When Wallace refuses this particular call to adventure, he is pushed even further when the next dramatic question is set up: Can William Wallace avenge the murder of his beloved wife? The answer to this dramatic question gives way to one of the most classic hero's journeys ever.

In *The Shawshank Redemption* Andy Dufresne (Tim Robbins) is convicted of murdering his wife and her lover. The initial dramatic question is asked: "Did Andy really do it?" When he reaches prison, this question becomes almost immaterial as our next question becomes: Will this white-collar worker survive the savagery of the prison environment? The rest of the film gives us a fascinating answer to both these questions. As a result, this film never dates and has become a perennial classic.

So, the protagonist has to confront the inciting incident or call to adventure in such a way that it leads to the **first plot point**,

twist or **turning point** at the end of Act 1. This turning point must create an even more dramatic situation than the initial set up of the story to ensure that the viewer is intrigued enough to stay the course for Act 2. This turning point is also referred to as **crossing the threshold**, in Vogler's terms, as the viewer must realise that there is no going back for the protagonist. The protagonist's journey is set into inevitable motion.

In Act 2 the protagonist attempts to resolve the dramatic question. This act is sometimes referred to as the **rising action**. All possibilities are explored in trying to solve the events set up by the inciting incident. In this act the protagonist has to find some way to deal with the antagonist and their forces which will try to stop our hero achieving their desires. The more believable and complex you make your antagonist and the greater their power to thwart your protagonist, the more compelling your story will be.

Many people's favourite movie characters are the villains. Characters such as Hannibal Lecter live on in the imagination forever. As I've said before, if he'd been any less powerful a character, *The Silence of the Lambs* would not be as unforgettable as film as it is now, even with Jody Foster's sterling performance. I also think the 2008 *The Dark Knight* Batman film would have been a complete yawn if it wasn't for Heath Ledger's brilliant portrayal of The Joker. In both these villains we have superb actors embodying brilliantly written antagonists.

To return to Act 2, our protagonist has to dig deep to find ways of overcoming the antagonist. They have to learn something, overcome weaknesses, face fears and demons to become more than they'd ever dreamt of. Usually they will need a mentor to help them succeed, or at least meet a few allies to help them along the journey.

Act 3 must finally answer the dramatic question and provide the audience with satisfactory solutions to all plot issues. The **resolution** or **pay off** must fulfil the questions asked in the set up. Every story strand should be tied up, especially if you are writing a classical hero's journey. The audience will feel cheated if their questions aren't answered adequately. So your **climax**, or **second turning point**, is of crucial importance.

This resolution of the dramatic question is ignored completely by filmmakers such as David Lynch, for example. His *Mulholland Drive* set out to confuse as many people as possible and it succeeded admirably.

Some scriptwriting teachers, such as Syd Field, believe you should know your ending before you start. It can be a great help if you do. I've written a few scripts where the only thing I was sure of at the start of writing was the ending. My task was to find the best way to get to that ending. I don't think it is always essential to know exactly the way your story will end, but you should have a reasonable idea of whether it will end well or badly for your hero. This will guide the choices you make along the way.

3. Recapping the Hero's Journey

I'm referring to the hero's journey blueprint here again to remind you of some of the best (in my opinion) teachers' structural frameworks. Have a look at it again on page 13.

4. In a Nutshell: As My Good Friend Emma Says ...

To conclude the whole question of structure as simply as possible, I'm going to leave the last word to my good friend, Emma Thompson. At least, I wish she was my good friend. I attended a scriptwriting workshop with Emma Thompson, Stephen Fry and Greg Wise when they visited South Africa some years ago. I spoke to Emma and Stephen privately afterwards for an article I was writing on the workshop and wished I could have gone home with them. It was truly a high point in my life.

During the workshop Emma quoted the brilliant director, Mike Nichols, who'd taught her one of the most important things she'd learnt about scriptwriting. He said that a writer (and a director obviously) had to set up a magnetic attraction at the beginning of the film and have the opposite pole of the magnet at the end, drawing one on relentlessly until the very last moment. I've remembered the image of the magnet ever since.

It's quite simple really. **Set up** your story with such a **powerful hook** right at the **beginning** of your film that a reader or viewer is drawn right to the very end by the magnetic attraction of the **resolution** or **pay off**.

Lastly, remember your choice of opening scene is pivotal. Start thinking about how you are going to start your script at this stage. Try to have some idea of how deep into the story you want to start your screenplay. American filmmakers have a saying about screenplay writing: "Start late and finish early". Start in the middle of the story so that the audience is instantly drawn into the journey. They must feel compelled to learn more.

TASKS

a. Watching films

1. Watch at least three of the classic films quoted above or any other classically structured films of your choice. See if you can identify Acts 1, 2 and 3, as well as the second turning points. Make notes of these scenes.
2. Watch *American Beauty* and see why this isn't a classic hero's journey. Does the different story structure affect the Act 1, 2 and 3 breaks? Are the turning points in the same place as they are for classic storytelling structures? Make notes of the progression of the acts and turning points.
3. Start working with your own story now. Is it easy to plot out Acts 1, 2 and 3 with very broad strokes? I want you to have a sense of where you'd like to break the narrative in terms of classic storytelling structure. Are you able to identify major turning points yet? If not, don't rush it. There is plenty of time to find these in Chapter 4. It's better to make a considered choice rather than a rushed one.
4. Play around with the broad strokes of your structure, which you drew up in the previous task. Can you swap the acts around? Could you start at the end, or would that be too confusing? Make sure that you have found the best possible points for a beginning, middle and end to your story.
5. Choose a number of films and examine their opening scenes. See how the scriptwriter chooses to start the story right in the middle of the action. Some of the recent modern films are better at this than some of the older ones. An excellent example of an opening scene starting right in the middle of the narrative is the film *Fur: An Imaginary Portrait of Diane Arbus*. Write down a few thoughts on the opening scenes you have watched.

b. Bonus Section for Advanced Screenwriting

Narrative Form in a Multiple-Protagonist Film

In classically narrated films, such as *Braveheart, Gladiator, Lawrence of Arabia* or *Erin Brockovich*, viewers are usually drawn in and compelled by the narrative because it is a classic hero's journey, in the Joseph Campbell sense. As such it fulfils all our requirements for story: a character we can **identify** with; a journey the hero must embark on to attain a goal; and the requisite number of setbacks, twists and believable turning points to keep our interest engaged. As Lajos Egri puts it: "Causation is the prime unifying factor in a classical narrative". Or to put it more simply: one thing leads to another in a single character's life in a classic story.

Usually the narration is told from a fairly restricted point of view with "the viewer in the best possible position – as the invisible observer" to events in mainly the central character's life, so that the character discovers things at the same time as the audience does.

Before we start to discuss multiple-protagonist narratives in more detail, let me refer you to one of the experts on this subject, Linda Aronson. She has written a number of brilliant books dealing with alternative scriptwriting, most notably *Screenwriting Updated* (2001) and *The 21st Century Screenplay* (2011).

Dealing with a less than classical story structure with a multi-stranded story woven into a tandem narration, I am compelled to ask this question: In a tandem narrative satire such as *Short Cuts* (1993) or *Crash* (2004), how can a viewer's interest be piqued and maintained and convey the inner states of the many, many characters? In other words, how can the screenwriter use the plot to unravel the story in a compelling way when there are so many characters to follow?

Take *Short Cuts,* Robert Altman's satirical film about Los Angeles, which explored the tandem narrative form. Before I talk about this film, here are the crucial elements of a tandem narrative as outlined by Linda Aronson:
- A tandem narrative tells several separate stories in the same film.
- It seeks to paint a large canvas with many different characters.

- Sometimes there are flashbacks.
- It's epic in aims and themes and wants to depict a whole community.
- It moves outward to represent an entire community.

Note that the tandem narrative is different to the sequential narrative as found in *Pulp Fiction*, for example. To clarify, the sequential narrative:
- It shows separate but interconnected stories, one after the other, linking them at the end.
- It shows more interest in the individual world and the viewpoint of each character to an event.
- It moves inward to show different views of the same event.

Read Linda Aronson's *Screenwriting Updated* for more explanations about tandem and sequential narratives.

Robert Altman's *Short Cuts*

If you have the good fortune to find a copy of Robert Altman's most creative film, in my opinion, try to examine how he constructed his tandem narrative in *Short Cuts*. Ask yourself how he connects us to the many very different characters in the film. Also, it's good to remember that this was the first time that we know of that such a vast, multi-stranded story was created *consciously* on film, even though television had used tandem narratives for years.

Firstly, Altman uses a compelling opening sequence – Los Angeles at night with helicopters flying overhead. The camera focuses on a sign lit up at one point in the opening sequence which warns us about the extremely dangerous med fly. The helicopters are spraying the city to destroy this terrible threat.

The opening scene cuts to a limousine driving under the helicopter's spray. Inside the limo, two drunken revellers are passing out in the back seat with a TV news report on the limo's TV. The broadcaster is talking about the dangers of the med fly. The driver of the limo leers at the drunks in the back as he drinks from a small bottle himself.

The voiceover by news reporter, Howard Finnegan, continues into the next scene: an upmarket house, then into the bedroom, to see Howard Finnegan himself watching the news broadcast about the dangers of the med fly. He calls his wife, Ann, who jumps onto the bed to watch the broadcast with him. She flicks through a magazine while asking Howard why he always wears his glasses on television. He doesn't show much irritation but is aware that she's not that interested in the broadcast. His words ring out ominously from the television screen: "Our objective is to destroy the med fly before it destroys us".

These words bleed over into the next scene, which cuts to a cello concert where the cellist is introduced as the next character in a strand of the narrative: Zoe. Two couples are watching the concert Zoe is performing. The doctor, Ralph, and his wife, Marian, are watching next to another couple, Stuart, a keen fisherman, and his wife, Claire. (We learn their names later.)

The next scene cuts back to the helicopters and then cuts to Jerry covering up his car, which has emblazoned on the side: "Jerry's Pool Care". Jerry looks up at the helicopters and decides to bring in the children's bikes. He carries them into his house. Inside, the children have the TV on, which is on the news broadcast about the med fly. His wife, Lois, is talking sexy for a client on the phone. She simulates phone sex with strangers while their children mill about. Jerry does not look happy.

We cut back to the helicopters again, which fly over a night club and a coffee shop. The singer from the club is heard in a voiceover. She's singing, "One day your man is with you. The next day he's gone … I'm a prisoner of life." (This scene foreshadows the scene with the limo driver and his wife. He's going to leave her soon too.)

The limo from the earlier sequence drives up to the coffee shop. The driver, Earl, gets out and goes in to have coffee with his waitress wife, Doreen. She's worried about whether he's been drinking again.

The camera pans out through the window to the helicopters again and the singer's voice gets louder. The camera zooms in to the night club where the singer is singing. We get a close-up of the singer: Tess. (We learn later that she's the mother of the cellist, Zoe, in the earlier scene.) The camera focuses on one of the tables, where another couple's story comes into focus. Bill and his partner, Honey, are drinking at a table with another couple whose house they're going to look after while they're away. Honey is Doreen's daughter.

The scene cuts to the helicopters again and then to the news broadcast about the med fly once more. The camera enters another home: Sherri, with her two small children, gets distressed about the med fly spray. She calls her husband, Gene, a traffic cop, to help her shut the windows. He puts the dog out under the spray, distressing the children and Sherri. He leaves in a fury. We've just been introduced to our eighth couple. And it's just the end of the credits!

There's still another couple who play a slightly more peripheral role – Betty Weathers and her ex-husband, Stormy. Altogether, that takes us up to nine couples. I'm including the cellist and her mother, the singer, as a couple here too, as their lives are profoundly changed by the end of the film. Holding on to all these narratives is quite a mammoth task for any writer as well as any director. But how do they make it possible for the audience to stay interested in all the stories?

This is where Robert Altman is masterful, especially in these opening scenes. He creates the external threat of the med fly to unite the characters under his microscope. Some respond to it more directly than others, but the constant presence of the helicopters in the opening scenes creates a unifying presence. The characters are under the same sky. They are all at risk from the apparent threat of med fly or the spray to kill the mysterious bugs. What is ironic, though, is that the med fly is a classic **McGuffin**. The McGuffin is a term Alfred Hitchcock, the famous director, coined to encapsulate something that seems to be of cosmic importance in the plot but is in fact a device used to stir up interest: a fake inciting incident if you like. The threat of the med fly is a red herring of classic proportions. We never hear about the med fly again once the story gets going.

So our omniscient narrator, an eye in the sky, personified by the helicopters in this film, shows us the lives of the many couples the narrative is going to explore. Our interest as an audience is piqued by the huge perceived external threat of med fly and the poison being used to kill them. A modern analogy would be the threat of the coronavirus and the rumours associated with the vaccines that are purported to help, but may carry hidden dangers. And so we are hooked – the story has drawn us in. What the plot is going to do over the next three hours – it's a very long film! – is to show us that the threat to each of the characters comes not from the med fly at all, but from the danger that lies within their homes, or sometimes, even within themselves. In fact, the premise of this film is that the monster within is more threatening than any monster outside.

With a multi-stranded plot like this it is a matter of some skill to weave the characters' stories together so that they automatically move from one character's life to the next. Altman does this by linking the couples' lives together inextricably, even though a character might not always be aware that their actions have affected someone else's life.

For example, the news reader, Howard Finnegan, and his wife, Ann, have a son, Casey, whom they adore. Casey decides to walk to school on the day before his birthday. Devoted mom Ann lets him walk so that she can order his birthday cake. Casey is hit by a car, driven by Doreen, the waitress at the coffee shop. At first, he seems alright and runs home. Doreen is so relieved that he isn't dead as she thinks it could have changed her life. She drives home to the trailer she shares with Earl. Ann comes home from ordering the birthday cake and sees Casey lying on the couch. He is soon unresponsive and rushed to hospital. The doctor called to work on his case is Ralph, the one half of a couple watching the cello concert earlier.

In this way, the viewer is constantly in touch with the characters and aware of the knock-on effect (pardon the pun) they might have on each other's lives without being aware of it themselves.

The director cuts from one scene to another just after we have received enough information about that particular character's story to keep us engrossed a little longer. The edits are done by linking from one scene to another with a recurring visual image. The helicopter shots are a prime example of this. Other examples are aural connections between scenes, such as when the song that Tess sings bleeds over into another scene, or when a siren from a police car passing Gene, the traffic cop, becomes a siren of an ambulance coming to the hospital. And then there are the causal connections. Claire, who works as a clown, comes into the hospital (where the dying Casey has his parents at his bedside) to entertain sick children. She meets up with two of the other characters by chance on her way to the paediatric ward.

Problems Writing Tandem Narratives

As seen above, we are drawn into the multi-stranded story by a skilful writer and director.

But there are a number of problems facing the writer of a tandem narrative. These have been documented as affecting sequential narratives and are listed as the following:
- How to get closure and meaning in the film?
- How to maintain pace within individual stories and the film as a whole?

- How to control the length of the film with the many story strands to attend to?

If you've seen *Short Cuts* you'll know that Altman didn't do too well with the third item on this list. I believe, though, that Altman managed to maintain the pace of the film by creating intriguing characters. We want to find out more about them, so we are prepared to do the work required to follow each story strand. Do bear in mind that this was the first film ever to tackle a multi-stranded story with a tandem narrative so deliberately. It is not as sophisticated as *Crash*, for example, but it was made 13 years before *Crash* and was ground-breaking in its time and is a classic and very effective satire in my opinion.

To clarify how *Short Cuts* is a satire I've provided notes on satire from two equally fascinating authors of scriptwriting, Ken Dancyger and Jeff Rush. Their book *Alternative Scriptwriting: Beyond Hollywood Formula Writing* (2013) is an invaluable guide to non-linear narratives. They state that satire is defined by the following points:

1. The central conflict relates to a crucial social or political issue of the day – environment, health care, the power of television, etc.
2. The film has a distinct point of view about the issue.
3. Humour mixes freely with aggression.
4. The central character is a vehicle to promote an issue.
5. Fantasy and unreality are acceptable in this free-form genre.
6. The level of aggression mounts rapidly, escalating to absurd levels before the film ends.
7. Relationships can only be transient, given the urgency of the posed social threat.
8. Random irrationality reminds us of the horror film. The genre succeeds when we see ourselves as victims of the danger and threat of society.
9. This is a vigorous and energetic genre and is not at all tied to realism, similar to the melodrama or film noir. High energy is rampant in these films.

After examining the various ways tandem narratives can be written, you can tackle the advanced tasks below if you're keen to embark on an alternative structure yourself.

c. Advanced Tasks

- Can you identify each character's story arc in a multiple-protagonist film such as *Crash, Pulp Fiction, American Beauty, Short Cuts* and *Little Miss Sunshine?* List one film's characters and plot out each character's story arc.
- Linda Aronson believes that multiple protagonists have character arcs that are only second act stories. Do you agree? If not, explain why not.

Recommended reading

Aronson, Linda. *Screenwriting Updated: New and Conventional Ways of Writing for the Screen*, Pan Macmillan, 2005.
Aronson, Linda. *The 21st Century Screenplay*. Alan & Unwin, 2010.
Dancyger, Ken and Rush, Jeff, *Alternative Scriptwriting*, Elsevier, 2007.

Chapter 4

THE PITCH IS THE THING ...

Writing a good pitch that encapsulates all the essentials of your script is one of the most important elements of scriptwriting. A pitch is the well-crafted summary you will use to sell your film to potential buyers. Writing the perfect pitch at this early point in the scriptwriting process ensures that the writer understands the controlling idea or moral premise behind the film before writing the rest of the script.

1. The Big Pitch-ure

The reason I feel quite confident about giving advice on pitching is that Jason Daniels of Fremantle Television UK told me after I had pitched at the marketing forum at Sithengi Film and Television Market some years ago that my pitch was one of the best pitches he'd heard. This was high praise indeed coming from someone of his stature as he must have listened to thousands of pitches over the years.

Writing a pitch is quite a skill. You need to be as succinct as possible and use language as powerfully as you can. A pitch is a selling document that will highlight the best aspects of your work to make it as marketable as you can. It is closer to an advertising pitch than it is to anything else. In the same way as advertising does, the pitch uses only words that will create the maximum effect. The words you use in your pitch have to be poetic. I often liken words in a pitch, poetry or advertising to being similar to condensed milk. Just as you dilute a spoonful of condensed milk to make a cup of milk, so should you use words in this instance. Cram as much condensed meaning as possible into each word. Use words that create as many levels of meaning as possible so that there are unconscious resonances in the reader or the listener. In a professional pitch, you have to appeal to the producers' imagination and use evocative words that create the mental image of what you are trying to sell. In advertising speak, you should "sell the sizzle, not the bacon".

2. Yes, But What is a Pitch?

To explain what I mean by a pitch I will clarify what I did in the verbal pitch Jason Daniels liked so much. It was a shortened version of one I'd presented to the South African Scriptwriters' Association, now the Writers' Guild of South Africa (WGSA), a few months earlier.

A Verbal Pitch

Although this pitch was verbal, I had spent weeks fine-tuning the written pitch, which I memorised beforehand. I was not going to leave anything to chance. I strongly suggest that you learn your verbal pitch verbatim too so that when the time comes for you to deliver the goods, even if you are terrified, you can draw on your memory. At the Sithengi verbal pitch I was given five minutes on stage with a full auditorium in a huge theatre. The VIP international producers were in the front row. I was alone on the stage. Fortunately, I had a microphone, so I didn't have to project too much. One thing I did know was that I had to grab their attention with everything I had in the few opening seconds on stage.

I began by telling the audience the best things about myself. I know it may sound immodest, but underplaying your skills in a forum like a pitching session is just plain stupid. You are there to sell yourself. No one will be the slightest bit interested in you if you say "Hi. I'm not a very good writer but I hope to get better." They'll be plugging their earbuds into their ears as you speak.

Start by listing your major achievements and highlight the things about yourself that make you unique. My best quality, I think, is that I am so damned prolific and can't stop writing. I emphasised that I had written many plays and screenplays. I also drew everyone's attention to the fact that my first produced play had attracted the attention of the esteemed critic, Stephen Gray, in his wrap of the Grahamstown Arts Festival that year in the *Mail & Guardian*. He'd mentioned *A Savage from the Colonies* first and said how compelling he'd found it.

I suggest that you use anything in your opening gambit that portrays you and your work in a positive light. Even if your writing style has been called strange and off-the-wall by a number of critics, put a spin on that and say that your screenplay has been called "inimitable and quirky". Make the most of your unique qualities without lying.

So I started the pitch with the introduction about myself, along the following lines:

> My name is Janet van Eeden. I am a produced playwright. I have written five screenplays, three radio plays and three stage plays. My last stage play was received with critical acclaim at the Grahamstown Arts Festival and it was called "ingenious" and "deeply engrossing" by the poet and critic Stephen Gray. He also mentioned it first in his wrap of the whole festival in the *Mail & Guardian*.

(This was many years ago and the number of stage plays and screenplays has increased significantly since then.)

I then went on to do a short pitch about the film itself. I punched it out with as much confidence and energy as I could muster. The way to do this is to imagine you are selling watermelons in a desert. Imagine that the panel are dying of thirst. You've got what they want. Believe it yourself and they will believe it too. Tantalise them with your pitch. And, always, the first part of the pitch consists of the tag line.

3. The Tag Line

Start the pitch with the tag line. I'm a great believer in the use of an excellent tag line as it's the short, pithy one-liner that sums up the essence of your film. A good tag line should entice producers to want to know more about your film.

Tag lines are also known as slug lines in America

A tag/slug line is something that sums up the whole moral premise behind your film/play in a snappy one-liner. Look at the back of DVD covers, if you have any, or even the back of best-selling novels. Often there are one-liners branded on the covers. Films usually put the tag line on their posters.

Classic one-liners include:

"In space, no-one can hear you scream." – *Alien*

"It will never be safe to go into the water again." – *Jaws*

"Look closer." – *American Beauty*

"A monster science created – but could not destroy." – *Frankenstein*

"There is a miracle in being young ... and a fear." – *Splendor in the Grass*

"A man went looking for America. And couldn't find it anywhere." – *Easy Rider*

"You don't make up for your sins in church. You do it on the streets." – *Mean Streets*

"On every street in every city, there's a nobody who dreams of being a somebody." – *Taxi Driver*

"Man has made his match ... now it's his problem," – *Blade Runner*

"Be afraid. Be very afraid." – *The Fly*

"Houston, we have a problem." – *Apollo 13*

"Never let your friends tie you to the tracks." – *Trainspotting*

"Can the most famous film star in the world fall for just an ordinary guy?" – *Notting Hill*

And from my own work:

"Dead men don't tell secrets." – *A Matter of Time*

"Roots run deep." – *In-Gene-Uity*

"Three women get savage, past, present and future." – *The Savage Sisters*

"He loves his women. To death." – *Expletive Deleted*

Think long and hard about the best possible tag line for your project. Use your moral premise as a guideline and play with words. I always advise scriptwriters to write down every thought that comes to them. You don't have to decide on a tag line immediately. It's often the last thing that comes to you in the writing process.

It's also a good idea to throw ideas around with a friend. Brainstorming is an excellent way to come up with something witty and sharp, and it's no surprise that advertising executives use it all the time.

When you've hit on the right tag line, you'll know. I always get goose bumps when the right tag line resonates with all I want to say in a film or a play. What I mean by "resonate" is when a phrase or word taps into the unconscious connections human beings have within us, the collective unconscious as Jung called it, either in a cultural way or in a universal way. This is what every writer should strive for: tap into a deep-seated universal vein in your audience and you will have a winner. Whether your themes are revenge, integrity, justice, love or whatever, this universal theme should come through in your pitch.

"Music was his life, but the army replaced it with a gun" sums up almost everything I want to say in my film about my brother, *A Shot at the Big Time*. It encapsulates that he was the ultimate artist who lived for his music, but he was forced to fight in a conscripted war that killed him. I'm not totally happy with this slightly long tag line but I will work on it until I get it even shorter. The essence of what I want to say is there, though, about the injustice meted out by an unfeeling authoritarian body. This is the universal theme I am tapping into.

The best tag line for *A Matter of Time* came to me years after I'd written it. Until then, I'd used "The only person you can trust with a secret is a dead one". That's the tag line I used on the poster when the play went to the National Arts Festival years ago. It worked well then and put across what I wanted to say, but the one I decided on above – "Dead men don't tell secrets" – is more succinct and catchier. However, both the first tag line and the final tag line convey that the story is about secrets and murder. That's the important message that I wanted to come across: this story is a murder mystery with perhaps a bit of revenge thrown in for good measure.

4. The Log Line

After you've found your tag line, you must come up with the longer **log line**. In South Africa, the United Kingdom and the USA there is a trend towards writing **a one-sentence synopsis** of the story and calling that the **log line**. That is then followed by a one-paragraph synopsis called the **one-paragrapher**, in the USA.

I have adopted the USA way of writing a pitch by using a **one-sentence log line** and then a **one-paragrapher** as each step reinforces the main themes of your story. It is also the preferred method of teaching a pitch in the top film schools in South Africa.

Both the short one-sentence log line and the one-paragrapher serve the same purpose. One is just a shorter version of the other.

Another screenwriting theorist, Blake Snyder, writes in his book, *Save the Cat: The Last Book on Screenwriting You'll Ever Need*, about the necessity to have a clear idea of whom the story is about in your log line. You have to be able to frame your story in this way:

"It's about a guy/girl who ..."

As Blake Snyder says again:

> *The "who" is our way in. We, the audience zero in on and project on to the "who", whether it's an epic motion picture or a commercial for a detergent. The "who" gives us someone to identify with and that someone doesn't even have to be human.*

To create the perfect protagonist, we have to have a **compelling** protagonist. This also goes for the antagonist.

Snyder suggests that a great log line (and one-paragrapher) is to have:
- An adjective to describe the hero
- An adjective to describe the bad guy
- A compelling goal we identify with as human beings.

Examples of good one-sentence log lines are the following:

"Two street-wise women break down in a small town and uncover a deadly secret between two backwoods brothers." *A Matter of Time*

"A hardened private eye discovers that a divorce case uncovers deception at the highest level in Los Angeles." – *Chinatown*

"He's a small-town rock star with a big-time future, but the army's about to smash his guitar with a gun." – *A Shot at the Big Time*

"A dysfunctional family is forced to go on a road trip to a beauty pageant and discover that they have more in common than they think." – *Little Miss Sunshine*

"An inauthentic family is forced to confront the emptiness of their lives and discover that the truth is not as bad as it seems." – *American Beauty*

As you can see, I have not always stuck to Blake Snyder's rule of putting an adjective before both the protagonist and the antagonist. I think words such as "deception," "the army" and "a beauty pageant" need no embellishment.

So for clarity and for my purposes, which encapsulate both the US's and the UK's current trends, in our pitch let us use the **one-sentence log line** and then the **one-paragrapher** after our **tag line**.

5. The One-Paragrapher or Short Synopsis

The one-paragrapher is the longer version of your one-sentence log line. As with all the other aspects of the pitch, you must use language as succinctly and as evocatively as possible. This one-paragrapher must encapsulate all the salient points in your screenplay. So it must contain the main character(s), their dilemma, the antagonist(s) and a sense of the direction the character(s) will take.

Here are some examples from three films I have written:

> "Nothemba walks the street for the first time wearing the pair of red patent leather sling-backs her mother brought home with so much hope. Her mother promised that these shoes would signal the start of the good times as they would make even the meanest punter dig deeper into his pocket. But the shoes didn't mean anything of the kind. Now the

too-big red shoes slip off Nothemba's plump feet as she walks the street looking for her first customer. Someone has to feed her brothers." – *The Red Shoes*

"The *Dunedin Star,* a British liner on its way to the Middle East, was shipwrecked along the Skeleton Coast on the 29th of November 1942. One hundred and six people were stranded on board a ship that was in extreme danger of breaking up in running seas. Forty-three of them made it to shore. The remainder were stranded on the wreck. This is the story of how the survivors were rescued from a coastline almost a thousand miles from the nearest habitable town. It is also the story of the trials faced by fearless men who crossed the sea and traversed virtually impenetrable land in a desperate race against time and the harshest coast imaginable to rescue the survivors. The difficulties they faced exceeded their worst nightmares. Neither the survivors of the wreck of the *Dunedin Star,* nor those brave men who risked their own lives to rescue them on the cursed Skeleton Coast, were ever the same again." – *Dunedin Star*

"Jimmy's family has personal crises instead of family holidays but he finds his soul in his music. Until the army sends him his call-up papers. He has to choose between following the rules or following his heart. He decides to sing his own tune. He steals a rifle and goes AWOL. Back home he gives the performance of his life, alternating guitar riffs with rapid rifle fire. Until he hears the sound no musician wants to hear: the sound of a dying woman. It seems the army will take its pound of flesh after all. Even if it costs Jimmy his life." – *A Shot at the Big Time*

In my opinion, the last two one-paragraphers above are the best, better even than the one I use below as the example of how to do a verbal pitch.

6. Putting it Together

To get back to the verbal pitch I did at Sithengi, here is an example of what I did.

After my initial statement about who I was and what I had achieved so far, I then gave them the tag line followed by the one-sentence log line:

> When there is nothing that man can do, a woman can make all the difference.
>
> *A Woman of Courage* is a true story of Sandra Brown (name changed for personal reasons) who risked everything to save the lives of AIDS orphans.

I did include the phrase that the film was *Erin Brockovich* meets *Mother Teresa* in the log line. A word of warning here, though. When I pitched my film a day after the marketing forum to a smaller Sithengi panel, one of the producers said that he hated this type of filmic shorthand. He said that he started thinking about the films mentioned rather than the one being pitched. Most of the producers agreed with him. They were all from Europe. Perhaps Europeans still don't like this Americanised way of doing things.

However, it is still up to you how you decide to pitch your story. As I said earlier, Jason Daniels from the UK thought my pitch was brilliant the day before. Remember that William Goldman said in his *Adventures in the Screen Trade*: "Nobody knows anything".

Next wrap up your film's story with a short and well-written one-paragrapher, something along the lines of the following:

> *A Woman of Courage* is the story of Sandra Brown, an ordinary woman who would not accept defeat. After suffering enormous emotional pain in her own life, including a rape, she comes across a village of AIDS orphans in Uganda. Horrified at the neglect of children who've been left to die alone, she vows to do something herself. She gives up her own home and takes in orphans and AIDS sufferers from all over KwaZulu-Natal.

> After years of financial hardship, she is given some assistance from the Nelson Mandela Children's Fund and enlists the help of a world authority on AIDS. She is finally given the recognition she deserves when she is invited to be a guest speaker at the World AIDS conference in 2000.

After you have given your brief outline, punch in a few more of your achievements or highlight the project's potential saleability. In the above example I would mention that Sandra's story has been covered in most of the national magazines. I would save, as the crowning glory, the fact that Danny Glover offered to help Sandra in any way possible when he heard her speak at the International AIDS conference.

So to sum up: start with your own achievements, go on to a punchy **tag line**, then the one-sentence **log line**, then in the **one-paragrapher** give a brief outline of the story.

End by listing any other interested parties who would like to be involved (the more high-profile, the better) and ask if there are any questions. If they want a more detailed outline be prepared to go into the minutiae of the events of the story. Remember to explain how the story will be SEEN on screen: try to describe the action of the film, not the character's internal musings. Be prepared to answer any questions they might throw at you. Questions are a good sign. It means they have not slept through your pitch, and they want to know more. When they are suitably impressed and satisfied, sashay out like a winner.

7. The Final Verbal Pitch

Here is the whole verbal pitch put together as one piece:

> My name is Janet van Eeden. I am a produced playwright. I have written five screenplays, three radio plays and three stage plays. My last stage play was received with critical acclaim at the Grahamstown festival and was called "ingenious" by the poet and critic Stephen Gray. He mentioned my play first in his wrap of the festival in the *Mail & Guardian*.

(Tag line)

When man can do nothing, ask a woman.

(One-sentence log line)

A Woman of Courage is a true story of Sandra Brown who risked all she possessed to save the lives of AIDS orphans.

(One-paragrapher)

A Woman of Courage is the story of Sandra Brown, an ordinary woman who would not accept defeat. After suffering enormous emotional pain in her own life, including rape, she comes across a village of AIDS orphans in Uganda. Horrified at the neglect of children who have been left to die alone, she vows to do something herself. She gives up her own home and takes in orphans and AIDS sufferers from all over KwaZulu-Natal. After years of financial hardship, she is given some assistance from the Nelson Mandela Children's Fund and enlists the help of a world authority on AIDS. She is finally given the recognition she deserves when she is invited to be a guest speaker at the World AIDS conference in 2000.

(Important facts)

Sandra Brown's story has been covered in most of the national magazines. When renowned actor Danny Glover heard her speak at the International AIDS conference, he offered to help her in whatever way he could. Enlisting him as an actor in the film would certainly boost its appeal.

Answer any questions they may have like a pro, and then sashay out like a winner.

8. What I Really Pitched

I used the example of Sandra Brown's story above because *A Matter of Time* was optioned for many years and so I couldn't write about it. The rights have since been released to me so now I can use it. Below is the actual pitch I used and it's much better than the example above.

This pitch is the one Jason Daniels thought was superb and which, when I pitched it to the South African Scriptwriters' Association/Writers' Guild of South Africa a few months before that, went down as one of the best pitches the panel had ever seen.

> My name is Janet van Eeden. I am a produced playwright. I have written five screenplays, three radio plays and three stage plays. My last stage play was received with critical acclaim at the Grahamstown festival and was called "ingenious" by the poet and critic Stephen Gray. He also mentioned my play first in his wrap of the festival in the *Mail & Guardian*.
>
> *A Matter of Time*: Two streetwise women break down in a small town and uncover a deadly secret between two apparently naïve brothers.
>
> *The only person you can trust with a secret is a dead one.*
>
> Two women from the city break down in a small town where people are apparently naive. They stay the night with two brothers whose unhealthy relationship explodes during a drunken game of Truth and Consequences. The consequences revealed by the truth are more than anyone can handle. In the morning there are too many bin bags on the pavement. And the bin men are late ... And the sun is getting hot ... And the dogs are beginning to gather ... It is only a matter of time.
>
> *A Matter of Time* was first written as a radio play and was short-listed by BBC World out of 1100 entrants into their final seven. Richard E Grant is keen to play the lead, and the producers, [Name Withheld], have just optioned the script.

The truth is that the screenplay went into six years of development hell, first with a South African production company and then with a British producer. This was the cause of the five years of turmoil I referred to earlier. I finally staged it as a play. Perhaps one day I'll make it as a film.

When I first pitched *A Matter of Time* at the Screenwriters' Association forum I mentioned earlier I was so nervous that I decided to fall back on my theatrical training. So I learnt the pitch by heart, brought in large photographs of the actors I wanted to play the lead roles and held these up whenever I referred to the characters they would portray in the film. I had also taken photographs in a little backwoods town, which would have been the perfect setting for my film. I held these up at appropriate moments.

I'd also brought in a large black bin bag, and placed it dramatically on the desk before I started my pitch. When I said: "The sun is getting hot" I simply patted the bin bag and left the rest to their imagination.

I hadn't seen any of the pitches before mine and had no idea that the others had just sat and talked during their pitches. As a result, I woke up the whole room. After the pitch was over, everyone asked me what was in the bag. They were convinced it was full of rotten meat. There was nothing of the sort in there. It contained only the towels I'd used during my weekend stay in Johannesburg. And they didn't smell at all. Their imagination had filled in the gaps, and I know it is immodest to say this, but the truth is that it's a pitch people have never forgotten.

9. The Written Pitch

I've written in great detail about the verbal pitch above because it is essentially the same as a written pitch. It also gives you the added skills of how to sell your film if you happen to bump into a producer at a party.

In a written pitch, however, the details of your own achievements and the assets you bring to the project will be included in your **statement of intent** when you write the **treatment** in Chapter 5.

The essentials of the pitch as I have outlined above are in fact the first part of writing the treatment. I like to make writers aware that the first part of their treatment is also the perfect pitch for their film. This is why I insist that you fine-tune it carefully as it serves a dual purpose.

TASK

Your single task in this chapter is to write the best pitch you can for your film. It is essential that you craft this pitch as carefully as possible. As you can see above, a slightly ordinary pitch can make your eyes glaze over. I don't think Sandra Brown's pitch is the best one ever written. I do think *A Matter of Time*'s pitch is excellent. The one-paragrapher for *A Shot at the Big Time* is also good, in my opinion. The reason that these two are good is because I spent weeks crafting each one to ensure that the pitches were as evocative as possible.

Your written pitch must include the following:

a. The tag line
b. The one-sentence log line
c. The one-paragrapher synopsis

While you are writing the pitch you must keep your moral premise at the forefront of your mind. This moral premise, controlling idea or theme must resonate in every word you write for your pitch.

Write your pitch as carefully and as succinctly as you can. Make sure that it really encapsulates the message you want an audience to take home with them.

Write it as evocatively as possible. Remember to sell the sizzle, not the bacon.

Recommended reading

Snyder, Blake. *Save the Cat: The Last Book on Screenwriting You'll Ever Need*, Michael Wiese Productions, 2005.

Chapter 5

THE RIGHT TREATMENT ...

A step-by-step guide to writing treatments (an internationally recognised film-selling document) that can be used anywhere in the film industry. Without knowing how to write a treatment, a scriptwriter will almost never sell a film.

What is a Treatment?

When I first started in the film industry years ago, I heard people at the top talking about writing something called "a film treatment". I was in awe of what I thought must be an extremely difficult and arcane piece of work. When I eventually discovered what a treatment was, I was amazed at what a simple document it is. Like all things, it's easy when you know how.

I must give credit to Julian Friedmann, my London literary agent, for unlocking the mysteries of writing treatments for me. I attended his pitching workshop at the Cape Town International Film Market, Sithengi, in 2001. While I was there, I bought his book: *How to Make Money Scriptwriting*, which has an excellent step-by-step guide on how to write treatments. I've used his guide over the years and adapted it as required for each project I've worked on. I now use a more updated version, which I've devised to suit my needs, and which is accepted throughout the industry internationally.

1. Where Do I Start?

The good news is that you have completed the first part of the treatment already by working on your pitch in Chapter 4. Fine-tuning your pitch is one of the most difficult aspects of writing a treatment. The opening few sentences of your treatment must be eye-catching and punchy and, if you have completed the tasks for your pitch satisfactorily, you will be close to successfully completing your treatment.

The treatment is essentially a summary of your film in attractive, bite-sized chunks which must appeal to the producer, director or agent who is reading this document. It must cover all the salient aspects of the script so that the filmmakers can glean all they need to know about the project and decide whether it appeals to them or not.

Remember that a treatment should be approximately three to five typed pages long. It should never be longer than five pages or the producers will feel swamped. The last thing you want to do is make them feel like you are wasting their valuable time.

Remember what Robert McKee said: "Brevity takes time. Excellence means perseverance". If you have written a flabby piece of work that rattles on for ten pages the producers will be very concerned that your screenplay will also be overwritten. As you will find out, verbosity is the enemy of a good screenplay.

Take time when writing your treatment to show off your writing ability. You must create a piece of work that lets the reader know that you are a powerful writer.

Once again, this is not the place for sloppy word usage and lazy writing. It is just as essential to be as succinct in your use of language as you were in your pitch. Continue the same poetic and evocative way of writing that you brought to the pitch when writing your treatment. It is your task to craft a finely tuned document to the best of your ability.

2. First Things First

Briefly, the treatment is a three- to five-page document that contains the following information about your film:
- Title
- Tag line
- One-sentence log line
- One-paragrapher
- Statement of intent
- Character biographies
- Synopsis

If you buy a copy of Julian Friedmann's book, you will see that I have adapted his basic framework. I include the one-sentence log line and the one-paragrapher so that it can be the basis of your pitch as well. He uses his treatments for novels as well as film so I prefer to go for the punchier American style of pitching a film, and I choose to include the tag line and one-sentence log line in the treatment.

You will notice that you have completed the first four steps of the treatment already by writing your pitch in Chapter 4. Now you have to continue writing throughout the rest of the treatment with the same intensity and focus.

Remember, huge-budget films are often sold on the quality of the treatment alone, often even before the script is written. Hollywood studios regularly option films in this way. Two of my writing students, who won the M-Net EDiT Grants when I lectured at the University of KwaZulu-Natal Pietermaritzburg for two years, won these grants on the strength of their treatments alone. Their scripts weren't written yet, but the quality of their treatments granted them access to funding to make their first films.

I also landed the prize job of writing the script for the multi-million-rand feature film *White Lion* purely on the strength of the treatment I submitted to the producers. There is no question that learning to write an excellent treatment is one of the most important things I can teach you in this book.

With much of your pitch written let's move on to working on your **statement of intent**.

3. Statement of Intent

The statement of intent is a feature that I choose to include when writing a treatment. Quite a number of American writers exclude this section, but I really believe it is important to let the producers know why YOU want to tell this particular story. This is the time to tell the producers about your own personal experience that qualifies you, especially, to write this film. A statement of intent should not be too long. A paragraph will often be enough to tell the producer where your inspiration came from.

If your story is a personal one, however, you may have to expand this section a bit more. You will see what I mean below.

Here are two examples of statements of intent that give you an idea of what is required from you. The first is from my play/screenplay *A Matter of Time*. It is taken from a treatment I did for producers who wanted to turn the play into a film for television. I had to give them the background to the whole story before they saw the script. To be honest, the statement of intent is a little long. However, it is a good example of what the producers want to hear from you:

> I wrote *A Matter of Time* after two factors collided in my imagination. The first was a trip to Grahamstown many years ago when my car, a Volkswagen Beetle, which had seen better days, broke down in the tiny town of Jamestown in the Eastern Cape. The car limped into Jamestown with smoke pouring out of the engine. At the only garage in this godforsaken town, I met characters exactly like the ones I later created in my play: Lucas, Mynhardt and Koos. The Lucas character took one look at the car and told me I needed a new engine, which could only be fetched from Queenstown the following day. As I was on my own, I asked whether there was a hotel where I could stay overnight. They pointed to a burnt-out pile of rubble. They laughed as they told me the hotel burnt down two years previously.
>
> After much anxiety, I ended up staying the night with the Mynhardt character and his wife. They were extremely kind although their house was in an appalling state of mess. The house was exactly like the one I describe in *A Matter of Time*.
>
> The man called Koos was "not all there", as the man called Mynhardt explained to me. Koos was very kind, though, and a bit infatuated with me. He told me a long story about "The Whistler", someone who would whistle late at night when women were alone in their homes. I thought this was a silly story as I really didn't think that someone whistling at night could be a threat in any way at all.
>
> That night, at Mynhardt's house, I learnt that Mynhardt and his wife had lived on the street for years. They'd finally decided to stay in a house when their two children were born. The local traffic cop came over that night to check me out too, and told me the story about the speed traps he set specifically for people travelling through their town.

> I went to sleep in the spare room, on a bed piled high with fluffy toys still in their cellophane wrapping. At about 1 o'clock in the morning, when it was pitch-dark outside, I was woken by a piercing whistle right outside my bedroom window. At that time of the night, in the pitch dark, it was the most terrifying sound I'd ever heard.
>
> The next day my stepfather drove into Jamestown to fetch me with a trailer to carry my Beetle back home. He and I were both surprised when my car started first time and never gave another moment's trouble.
>
> Years later, I dreamt about two women breaking down in a small town and staying overnight with two single brothers. In the dream the women goaded the brothers to expose a dark secret of theirs through a game. In the dream I saw the black bags full of body parts on the pavement in the morning. So I decided to put the story of the dream and the reality of my experience in Jamestown together, and *A Matter of Time* was born.

As I said earlier, this statement of intent is definitely too long, but the genesis of this story is quite interesting, I believe. Everyone who has read this treatment so far seemed to find the background to this story intriguing.

Here is another statement of intent that is part of the treatment for the film *A Shot at the Big Time*. Remember, this is a very personal story about the life of my brother and his death on the border during the South African Border Wars. It is also longer than most statements of intent, but I believe it is important to let any producer reading this particular treatment know that this film is based on a true story.

> *A Shot at the Big Time* is the true story of my brother, in particular, and about the futility of war in general. I have used my brother's story, which is Oedipal in its tragic intensity, to focus on the senselessness of the South African Defence Force's (SADF) conscription campaign during the 1970s and 1980s in this country. This film will include in its compass the experience of one soldier in uMkhonto weSizwe (MK), the

military wing of the ANC. It is an anti-war film in the classic tradition of *Apocalypse Now, Platoon, Born on the Fourth of July, M.A.S.H.* and *Catch 22*, among others. It is also a tirade against cruel authority and fundamentalism. For this reason, *One Flew Over the Cuckoo's Nest* is also an inspiration I used when writing this film.

The only thing Jimmy, my brother, didn't want to do was to kill another human being. The terrible irony is that by trying to defy the army and its constrictions, he broke the rules and went AWOL, taking a rifle with him to give the finger to the forces in the way he thought best. Through a series of random coincidences, an innocent woman was killed by a ricochet bullet from his rifle when he and his friends were firing into the local rubbish dump. This event was too much for him to bear and he had a mental breakdown. He was put into a mental institution for months. But it didn't take long for the army to reclassify him as fit to serve on the border. When he was sent to the border, a staff sergeant forced him to engage in active combat against his will. Three days after his arrival on the border, he was dead. Official reports said he was killed by a ricochet bullet. I believe, and people who were on the border at that time told me, that he shot himself rather than engage in active combat.

I would like to tell his story and that of all those young men, many of them who were only 17 like my brother, who were conscripted into a war to which many of them weren't committed. Many South African men are still suffering severely as a result of what they went through during the apartheid border war. Every person I've spoken to who has been through this war has urged me to tell this story.

The above statement of intent comes from the heart, and I've been as honest as possible in talking about this film. One of its strongest selling points is that it is based on a true story. A less personal story would not require as much detail, but producers want to know that a story is about something meaningful to you as a writer. I believe that the more passionate you are about a story, the more a producer will care about reading it. There are thousands of stories out there. Remember that you want to convince a producer that **YOU** are the only person qualified to tell this particular story.

The statement of intent should explain the reasons behind the writing of your film. To reiterate, the best treatments are between three to five pages long in total. If you spend a page and a half writing your statement of intent, you'll have fewer pages left to describe the characters and the storyline.

4. Character Biographies

This section gives the reader a sense of who the main characters are in the screenplay. Once again it is vital to give only a few salient points about each character. Do not go into elaborate detail about your character's **back story** at this stage. By **back story** I mean all the underlying storylines that won't necessarily make it onto screen but that made your character become who they are when we meet them. You will have written detailed character breakdowns for yourself in the process of writing the screenplay, I hope, but which you will just hint at here. Just describe a number of vital elements that will illustrate why this character will be compelling to watch on screen.

For a treatment of three to five pages, you need write only approximately three or four sentences about each character. Only include characters who affect the course of the storyline. I'll repeat this: do not include every single character mentioned in the screenplay. Only those who are pivotal to the storyline must be included.

I have a personal rule of thumb about character biographies. I never like to include more than ten characters in a character bible. The fewer, the better. I think that a reader can only absorb so many facts in one go, and bombarding the reader or producer with intricate back stories about every character mentioned in the screenplay will make them lose interest.

Once again, I'll give you a few examples from my work. *A Matter of Time* is an ensemble piece in which the story is driven only by the characters. I had to describe each of the eccentric characters in some detail as all of them play a crucial role in the plot. My task here was to give as much information as I could so that the synopsis would make sense.

Sarah: a white woman in her thirties or forties. She's a hard-bitten city woman, highly intelligent, and very bitter towards men. She doesn't suffer fools gladly and has no qualms about embarrassing people by showing up their inadequacies. Like all bullies, she is in fact hurting more than anyone else. She was raped by her father when she was a very small girl.

Cassie: a black woman in her early thirties or forties. She's an intelligent young woman, and has big plans for the future. Sarah has taken her under her wing at the school where they both teach. Although she's independent and strong, Cassie doesn't mind going along with the flow. She's very compassionate and can relate to most people, even to Koos, who has an intellectual disability. It is this quality that makes Mynhardt infatuated with her.

Lucas van Schalkwyk: a white man in his about mid-forties or more. Not educated beyond Standard Seven, he is a product of his racist past. He is not impressed to find that a black woman is going to stay in his house, but he goes along with the situation to see if he can find some sort of entertainment in the set-up. Lucas is mean-spirited, mainly because he is jealous of his gentle younger brother, Mynhardt. Even as a child his mother preferred Mynhardt to him, so he spent his life finding ways to torment his brother. He has relied on Mynhardt's kind-heartedness through the years to allow him to continue his domination of the garage, the house and their lives.

Mynhardt van Schalkwyk: a white man in his forties. He is Lucas' brother. He is a gentle-hearted person who always sees the best in others, even in his brother. It takes an enormous amount to get him angry. We only see this anger when Sarah pushes him to the limit of his endurance. He always has a home for waifs and strays and cares deeply for Koos. He is attracted to Cassie because her gentle nature reminds him of Marta.

Koos: a young Coloured man of about nineteen. He's intellectually disabled and stays very close to Mynhardt, whom he sees as his protector. He loves Mynhardt with his life and would do anything for him. He is the voice of truth in the script. Just as Shakespeare would use the fool to say the unthinkable, so Koos says the most pertinent things in the play. His innocence allows him to see situations clearly.

Poppie: the daughter of the local butcher, a no-nonsense white woman in her early forties. She has seen the lives of people evolving in the town over the years from her vantage point of the shop. She knows more than anyone what is really going on behind closed doors. She also realises immediately that the two women from the city are going to cause trouble. She is married to Frans and has looked after Koos since he was born.

Frans: the local traffic cop, white and mid-forties. He is married to Poppie. He's not very bright, but covers his stupidity with crude bluster. He and Lucas get on well because they love to make fun of Koos together. He likes to pretend he is as strong as an ox. Although he may be physically strong, he crumbles in the presence of Poppie. Even though Frans isn't too happy about Koos living with him and Poppie, he has to make the best of It. After all, Poppie is the boss in their home.

Flashbacks

Klaas: a black man in his late twenties. He was a gardener who lived with his parents on the property in Poppie's parents' garden. He and Poppie grew up together. There is a hint that something more went on between Poppie and Klaas, and the audience should be led to believe that Koos might be the product of their illicit relationship.

Marta: a young black girl of 16 who came to work as a maid for the Van Schalkwyks to help support her family. Terrified of being among strangers, she warmed to Mynhardt, who was only a little older than she was then. They spent all their time together when she wasn't working. It didn't take long for them to fall in love. When Lucas followed them into the veld one day, he saw them making love and was so jealous, he insisted that Marta have sex with him too. Marta was soon pregnant and kept the fact hidden from the boys' parents. When she went into labour, she was too afraid to call anyone, so she gave birth in her room. When they found her, she was dead, and the baby was barely alive. He was oxygen-deprived and brain-damaged. Koos was the baby.

As you can see, the treatment for *A Matter of Time* will definitely be one that will stretch to five pages. It was important to include the two characters from the flashback because they are the cause of the outburst during the drunken game of Truth and Consequences. Their role in the drama is pivotal. Giving information about them in the character biographies alerts the reader to the fact that their stories will be explored in the synopsis.

It is important to note here that these two characters in the flashback aren't even mentioned in the one-paragrapher. They are merely hinted at in the sentence: "The consequences of the truth are more than anyone can handle ..."

Here is another set of character biographies from the film *A Shot at the Big Time*. One again I've included many characters as they are pivotal to the unfolding of the narrative.

> **Jimmy:** a white 17-year-old boy from a dysfunctional home. Father is an alcoholic with an aversion to paying bills and they move from pillar to post, always just one step ahead of the debt collectors. Jimmy seeks refuge from the lack of positive role models in his harsh life by immersing himself in his music. He is a gifted guitarist and wants to be a rock star until he is conscripted into the army. His hatred of the army is compounded by the brutal treatment he receives from one of the officers in command. The only problem is that the army holds all the aces.
>
> **Jess:** Jimmy's adoring younger sister (15), who bears witness to the events.
>
> **Jimmy's father, Frank:** a white, well-meaning alcoholic (40-something) man who can't support his family although he always means to do better. He takes his frustrations out on Jimmy, by beating him and anyone else who gets in his way.

Jimmy's mother, Mary: a woman (early forties) who is overwhelmed by her circumstances. She doesn't have the self-esteem or the power to change the circumstances around her, even when she needs to help her son the most. Her children are everything to her and she loves her son, Jimmy, especially. She watches helplessly as he is brutalised by first his father, then the army.

Petrus: a 17-year-old black man who grew up with Jimmy. He spends time with Jimmy and the band whenever he can escape the watchful eyes of the apartheid system. He teaches Jimmy to play the guitar when they are both young. Initially, they have only their love of guitar-playing in common, but they soon discover they both have alcoholic fathers. And both have a deep passion for music that supersedes everything else in their lives. When Jimmy is forced to join the army and the tragic accident happens where Petrus' sister is killed, he takes his indigenous name, Vuyo, and decides to join MK. Jimmy's story in the SADF parallels Vuyo's experiences in uMkhonto weSizwe.

Band members, Gio: (20) a young white man who has avoided the army through having Italian citizenship and having wealthy parents. He sticks by Jimmy until the girl is killed. Then he and the other band members abandon Jimmy.

Band member, Rocky: a childhood friend of Jimmy's and Jess', and now a member of the band.

Band member, Sam: a friend of Jimmy's and a member of the band. He is a happy-go-lucky boy from a fairly ordinary background who joins the band for the fame and the girls.

Neliswa: Petrus/Vuyo's sister (16) who has a crush on Jimmy and tries to watch the band play during their alternative concert on the rubbish dump. It is her unfortunate fate to be in the wrong place at the wrong time.

Wiese: a corporal in the army (thirties) who is takes an instant dislike to Jimmy because he is English-speaking and because he is a musician. He soon makes it his life's work to terrorise Jimmy, especially when Van Staden seems to take Jimmy under his protective wing.

Van Staden: commanding officer (forties/fifties) in the camp where Jimmy is sent to do his basic training. Initially he likes Jimmy very much when he discovers Jimmy is a musician. He sets out to befriend him. He is a sensitive man trapped in an unhappy marriage, but he soon shows Jimmy he wants more than friendship. Jimmy has to decide whether Van Staden's price for an easy ride through the army is worth paying. But when Jimmy doesn't succumb to Van Staden's seduction, Van Staden makes him pay the ultimate price for being a rebel.

Martins: a kindred spirit in the army who befriends Jimmy in the barracks. Both are of English descent and are branded "Souties" – salt dicks – with one foot in England and the other in South Africa. So they stick together to try to find some sort of sanity in the army.

Gerhard: a traditional Afrikaner Nationalist who comes to the army to do the right thing and follow orders. However, even he finds that the army has no logic and he is side-lined by his own "volk". He finds that the Englishmen or "Souties" are far more to his liking than he'd first thought.

There are more than ten characters in the above biography, I'm afraid, but I thought it was worth including them all because of the nature of this epic feature film. As a writer, you have to keep reinforcing the salient aspects of the storyline throughout the treatment. Include the aspects of the characters you are describing that show how their roles play out in the plot.

5. Synopsis: Telling the Story

So far in the treatment you have concentrated on selling the story and giving a few tasty hints about where it is going. The synopsis is the part of the treatment where you have to deliver what you have promised. It's all very well to sell the sizzle in the early part of the treatment, but now you have to make sure that the sizzle you have sold the reader comes from real bacon and not a vegetarian alternative.

Once again it is important to tell the story you have set up over the past few pages of your treatment in as appealing a way as possible. Your **synopsis** or **summary** of the story should follow the basic hero's journey which you covered in Chapter 1. In other words, you must write the synopsis by adhering to good storytelling practices.

Once again, this is the time you write evocatively and succinctly, but using good story-telling techniques. Keep the reader engaged while you write. Do not waffle or get side-tracked. Keep to the main story turning points which you should have worked out in Chapter 3. This is not the time for introspection about the character's motives or possible outcomes if they had acted differently. This is the time to cut to the chase. As your time for giving scriptwriters seductive hints about the storyline is over now, you have to tell the producers exactly what they can expect to SEE in this film.

Without writing a blow-by-blow description of every event in the film, you describe the arc of the main character, the journey they go on, which you explored through the hero's journey, and you have to tell the producers what happens in the end.

I will use the two films I have been working on again to give you two examples of synopses. *A Matter of Time* should be quite familiar to you now, as you've been fed bite-sized chunks of the story through the pitch and the character biographies so far. See if the synopsis lives up to your expectations.

A Matter of Time – Synopsis

> Sarah and Cassie, two teachers from an upmarket Johannesburg school, are driving towards the arts festival in Grahamstown. When their ancient Volkswagen Beetle starts spewing smoke,

they manage to limp into the only garage in Georgetown, a town whose inhabitants are straight out of *Paris, Texas*.

There are three men outside the garage. They are the brothers, Mynhardt and Lucas van Schalkwyk, and Mynhardt's friend, Koos. Mynhardt tells the women a little later that Koos is "not all there".

Lucas spots his main chance to make some money and tells the women their car is irreparable. According to him they will have to wait until he can get a new engine from Queenstown, a town some distance away. This will take at least a day. He assures them there is no other alternative. He phones his friend, Pieter, in Queenstown to arrange for a new engine to be delivered in a day or two.

When the women find out that the only hotel burnt down two years earlier and there is nowhere for them to stay, they are devastated. Especially when Koos tells them about "the whistler", a character who apparently scares women by whistling outside their bedrooms late at night when they are alone at home.

The ever-kind Mynhardt asks Lucas if the women can stay at their house. Lucas agrees reluctantly. The women, Koos and Mynhardt take their bags to the house. It is filthy: cigarette posters "from the reps" stuck on the wall, newspapers piled everywhere, kittens splashing in milk under the kitchen table and new-born puppies in the bathroom. Sarah is disgusted but Cassie is too polite to show any disdain.

Mynhardt is fascinated by Cassie, which upsets Sarah. Sarah decides she needs a lot of alcohol to get her through the night. Especially when Cassie seems less than delighted with Sarah's sexual overtures when they discuss sharing a bed in the spare room. They go to the only shop in the town where cat food and KY Jelly share shelf space. Poppie runs the shop. She is not happy with these women coming into her town. She treats them with deep suspicion. Sarah buys up all the supplies of liqueur, almost past its sell-by date, and as much brandy as she can afford.

They return to the house laden with alcohol. Lucas returns, and they are soon joined by the local traffic cop, Frans, Poppie's husband. He is keen to show off in front of the new ladies in his town. As there is nothing else to do, all of them drink steadily.

Sarah becomes drunker and also more jealous of Cassie by the minute especially as Cassie seems quite taken with the gentle Mynhardt. Sarah initiates a game of Truth and Consequences to alleviate her boredom. Seething quietly, Sarah elicits Lucas' ill nature to side with her in her bitter attack on Mynhardt and Cassie and anyone who gets in her way in the vicious game.

Sarah's sharp intelligence quickly senses deep tension between the two brothers. She is relentless in her probing questions and soon unearths a dark secret the brothers have kept hidden for years: Marta, a young black girl Mynhardt had loved deeply, had been raped by Lucas. She died giving birth to Koos, and the oxygen-deprived baby was brought up by Poppie. Koos is either Lucas or Mynhardt's child.

Excited, jealous, drunk and angry at Cassie and Mynhardt, Sarah loses it completely and goads Mynhardt into taking his revenge on his brother for the terrible thing he'd done to Marta years before. In a fit of rage, Mynhardt kills Lucas.

As the sobering reality sets in, Sarah falls apart. Poppie arrives to look for her husband, and finds Lucas's body instead. Never one to flinch from a crisis, especially as she's a butcher's daughter, Poppie decides to solve the problem in the way she knows best. She sends the two hysterical women to the bedroom and calls on the men to help her remove the evidence.

In the morning, there are too many bin bags lining the pavement. The sun is getting hot. The bin men are on strike and the dogs are beginning to gather ... The truth will out. It is only a matter of time ...

And that is when Pieter, from the garage, arrives from Queenstown with the new engine. He's looking for Lucas.

Hopefully this synopsis will give you an idea of how to tell your own story with broad strokes. *A Matter of Time* is not an action film as it takes place in one night and a day and the actions arise out of a verbal game. It's not so easy to show what will be SEEN on screen. Instead, I had to explain the reactions of characters to the words and behaviour of their fellow characters as the action of this drama comes out of reactions of the characters.

In my opinion, the above synopsis is not quite as well-crafted as the synopsis of *A Shot at the Big Time*. See what you think. Here is *A Shot at the Big Time*'s synopsis.

A Shot at the Big Time – Synopsis

Jimmy is a rock star and his groupies are mad about him. All 13 of them. That's because Jimmy plays lead guitar for *The O.D. Boys,* a group of rock star wannabes in the Free State town of Odendaalsrus. Petrus, the township boy who gets drafted in as the band's roadie, cements a friendship with Jimmy as they share shattered lives and strong joints. Petrus taught Jimmy to make a guitar out of an old oil tin when they were both small boys. Their dreams grow with their skills. Petrus hopes that maybe he too can become a rock star. And when the authorities aren't looking, Petrus picks up the guitar and plays in the band too.

An agent from the big city hears the band play and Jimmy's world blasts into orbit. With a record deal (and some anonymous love letters) in his top pocket, Jimmy's about to hit the Big Time. Until the postman brings him his army call-up papers.

And so he starts the jail sentence that is National Service in the South African Defence Force. A corporal called Wiese has a bullet with Jimmy's name on it. He sets out to break his spirit.

Undergoing brutal training in the fine art of killing, Jimmy finds that his sensitive soul is getting de-tuned.

Until a commanding officer called Van Staden sets out to rescue Jimmy from Wiese's brutality. Van Staden is a fellow musician and feels an affinity for Jimmy's sensitive spirit. He takes him under his wing, driving Wiese into an even more impotent fury.

However, there is no such thing as a free lunch, and Van Staden soon lets Jimmy know the price he has to pay for his protection. Van Staden wants a little more than platonic friendship. Jimmy is shocked. He tries to let Van Staden down gently. But hell has no fury as a commanding officer scorned. It is only a matter of time before Van Staden takes away Jimmy's guitar and his first weekend pass, the one which would have seen him recording his first track with the record company.

So Jimmy breaks the rules. All of them. The worst of them. He goes AWOL. But not before he has stolen back his guitar, and – to show Van Staden what he really thinks of him – an R1 rifle with many rounds of ammunition.

When Jimmy gets home, he hears that the recording session has been cancelled. He almost loses heart. Until he decides to play anyway. Alternating guitar riffs with rapid rifle fire, he and his fellow band members stage an impromptu concert at the local rubbish dump. They give the performance of their lives.

Petrus hears that Jimmy is back, and he and his sister, Neliswa, the author of the pink love letters, decide to watch him play. Neliswa shyly hides near some debris on the rubbish dump while Petrus hops up on stage to accompany the band with his tin guitar.

Suddenly a scream is heard. One of the bullets ricocheted off an old fridge and punctured the heart of Neliswa. In panic, the rest of the band members flee, leaving Jimmy to face the music of Petrus's grief alone. That is when Jimmy learns that Neliswa is the author of his love letters and Petrus decides that his father is right after all: all whites are his enemy.

The back-up vocalist, Sam, runs to the cops and sings like a canary. When Jimmy realises what he has done, he has a mental breakdown. He is arrested by the military police and Van Staden chooses to throw him into "The Nutcracker Suite", the psychiatric unit dedicated to getting shell-shocked soldiers back into action. Whether they like it or not.

When Jimmy is finally discharged from active duty, nobody wants to know him anymore. Worse than that, he can't seem to get the music to flow from his fingers again.

Meanwhile, Petrus has changed his name to Vuyo and joined uMkhonto weSizwe, determined to fight for his freedom against whites who are now his enemy.

That is when Jimmy gets "re-volunteered" by Van Staden to be one of an elite squad of trained maniacs who will go on seek-and-destroy missions on the Angolan border. Even though Jimmy pleads and begs, his bags are packed for him, and he is waved off at the station by his parents and his last remaining fan, his little sister, Jess.

Against his will, Jimmy is forced to go on a mission into enemy territory. He jumps out of the Bedford truck with the rest of the soldiers, but instead of firing at will, he releases all the magazines of bullets from his rifle. As he walks out into the veld on his own, with enemy fire ringing around his ears, he strums his rifle as if it were a guitar. He walks straight towards a group of MK cadres.

Before Jimmy sees them, Vuyo recognises his old friend. He tells his comrades to hold their fire. For a long, long moment, he stares at Jimmy, his rifle pointed towards his heart. Then Jimmy sees his friend in the bushes and is broken at the sight of him. He drops to his knees and begs him to shoot him. Vuyo hesitates, about to walk towards Jimmy who is still begging to be shot when one of the other cadres shoots a hail of bullets deliberately into Jimmy's body. Vuyo is distraught. He grabs the dying Jimmy, who thanks him for putting an end to it all. As Jimmy dies in his arms, the only thing that matters to either of them is their childhood friendship.

Van Staden phones Jimmy's family to tell them their son and brother has been killed by a ricochet bullet. His family will never be the same again.

This synopsis is longer than the one for *A Matter of Time* as it spans a number of years and a few huge events. I think it is important to include everything as every single event is pivotal to the plot line. Hopefully, it is fast-paced enough so that the producer reading this will visualise the very dramatic events as they unfold.

6. Writing Your Treatment

Your task in this chapter is to write your own full treatment. Using your pitch as the first section of the **treatment**, complete your **statement of intent**, the **character biographies** and the **synopsis** with the same intensity and focus you brought to writing the **pitch**. Concentrate on telling a good story. If your treatment reads like a cracking good yarn, you will have no trouble selling it to a producer or a director. This is one of the most important lessons I can teach you, as I mentioned earlier, so give this task your best attention.

Your treatment should look like the treatments that follow, not much more than five pages, and in the same format as set out below. Write your treatment to the best of your ability. It is one of your most important tasks thus far.

Treatment of *A Matter of Time*

Dead men don't tell secrets.

The only person you can trust with a secret is a dead one.

Two streetwise women from the city break down in a small town where people are apparently naive. They stay the night with two brothers whose unhealthy relationship explodes during a drunken game of Truth and Consequences. The consequences revealed by the truth are more than anyone can handle: too many bin bags on the pavement in the morning. The secrets of the past are beginning to smell. And the bin men are late ... and the sun is getting hot ... and the dogs are beginning to gather. It is only a matter of time ...

Statement of Intent

I wrote *A Matter of Time* after two factors collided in my imagination. The first was a trip to Grahamstown many years ago when my car, a Volkswagen Beetle which had seen better days, broke down in the tiny town of Jamestown in the Eastern Cape. The car limped into Jamestown with smoke pouring out of the engine. At the only garage in the godforsaken town I met characters exactly like the ones I later created in my play: Lucas, Mynhardt and Koos. The Lucas character took one look at the car and told me I needed a new engine, which could only be fetched from Queenstown the following day. As I was on my own, I asked whether there was a hotel where I could stay overnight. They pointed to a burnt-out pile of rubble. They laughed as they told me the hotel burnt down two years before.

After much anxiety, I ended up staying the night with Mynhardt and his wife. They were extremely kind although their house was in an appalling state of mess. It was exactly like the one I described in *A Matter of Time*.

Koos was also "not all there", as the Mynhardt explained it. He was very kind, though, and a bit infatuated with me. He told me about "The Whistler", someone who would whistle late at night outside of the bedrooms of women who were alone in their homes. I didn't think that someone whistling at night could be a threat in any way.

That night, at Mynhardt's house, I learnt that Mynhardt and his wife had lived on the street for years. They'd finally decided to stay in a house when their two children were born. The local traffic cop came over to check me out too, and told me the story about the speed traps he set especially for passers-by.

I went to sleep on the bed in the spare room, amid piles of fluffy toys still in their cellophane wrapping. At about 1 o'clock, when it was pitch dark, I was woken by the most piercing whistle right outside my bedroom window. It was the most terrifying sound I'd ever heard.

The next day my stepfather came to fetch me with a trailer to carry my Beetle back home. He and I were both surprised when my car started first time and never gave another moment's trouble.

Years later, I dreamt about two women breaking down in a small town and staying overnight with two single brothers. In the dream the women goaded the brothers to expose a dark secret of theirs through a game. In the dream I saw the black bags full of body parts on the pavement. So I decided to put the story of the dream and the reality of my experience in Jamestown together, and *A Matter of Time* was born.

Character Biographies

Sarah: a white woman in her late thirties or early forties. She's a hard-bitten city woman, highly intelligent, and very bitter towards men. She doesn't suffer fools gladly and has no qualms about embarrassing people by showing up their inadequacies. Like all bullies, she is in fact hurting more than anyone else. She was raped by her father when she was a small girl.

Cassie: a black woman in her early or mid-thirties. She's an intelligent young woman, and has big plans for the future.

Sarah has taken her under her wing at the school where they both teach. Although she's independent and strong, Cassie doesn't mind going along with the flow. She's very compassionate and can relate to most people, even to Koos who is intellectually disabled. It is this quality that makes Mynhardt infatuated with her.

Lucas: a white man of about 40 or more. Not educated beyond Standard Seven, he is a product of his racist past. He is not impressed to find that a black woman is going to stay in his house, but he goes along with the situation to see if he can find some sort of entertainment in the set-up. Lucas is mean-spirited, mainly because he is jealous of his gentle younger brother, Mynhardt. Even as a child his mother preferred Mynhardt to him, so he spent his life finding ways to torment his brother. He has relied on Mynhardt's kind-heartedness through the years to allow him to continue his domination of the garage, the house and their lives.

Mynhardt: a white man in his early forties. He is Lucas' brother. He is a gentle-hearted person who always sees the best in others, even in his brother. It takes an enormous amount to get him angry. We only see this anger when Sarah pushes him to the limit of his endurance. He always gives a home to waifs and strays and cares deeply for Koos. He is attracted to Cassie because her gentle nature reminds him of Marta.

Koos: a young Coloured man of about nineteen. He's intellectually disabled and stays very close to Mynhardt, whom he sees as his protector. He loves Mynhardt with his life and would do anything for him. He is the voice of truth in the script. Just as Shakespeare would use the fool in his plays to say the unthinkable, so Koos says the most pertinent things. His innocence allows him to see situations clearly.

Poppie: the daughter of the local butcher, a no-nonsense white woman in her early forties. She has seen the lives of people evolving in the town over the years from her vantage point of the shop. She knows more than anyone what is really going on behind closed doors. She also realises immediately that the two women from the city are going to cause trouble. She is married to Frans and has looked after Koos since he was born.

Frans: the local traffic cop, white and mid-forties. He is married to Poppie. He's not very bright, but covers his stupidity with crude bluster. He and Lucas get on well because they love to make fun of Koos together. He likes to pretend he is as strong as a bull, and although he may be physically strong, he crumbles in the presence of Poppie. Even though Frans isn't too happy about Koos living with him and Poppie, he has to make the best of it. After all, Poppie is the boss in their home.

Flashbacks

Klaas: a black man in his late twenties. He was a gardener who lived with his parents on the property in Poppie's parents' garden. He and Poppie grew up together. There is a hint that something more went on between Poppie and Klaas, and we are led to believe that Koos might be the product of their illicit relationship.

Marta: a young black girl of 16. To support her family, she came to work for the Van Schalkwyk's as a maid. Terrified of being among strangers, she warmed to Mynhardt who was only a little older than she was then. They spent all their time together when she wasn't working. It didn't take long for them to fall in love. When Lucas followed them into the veld one day, he saw them making love and was so jealous, he insisted that Marta have sex with him too. Marta was soon pregnant and kept the fact hidden from the boys' parents. When she went into labour, she was too afraid to call anyone, so she gave birth in her room. When they found her, she was dead, and the baby was barely alive. He was oxygen-deprived and brain-damaged. Koos was the baby.

Synopsis

Sarah and Cassie, two teachers from an upmarket Johannesburg school, are driving towards the National Arts Festival in Grahamstown. When their ancient Volkswagen Beetle starts spewing smoke they manage to limp into the only garage in Georgetown, a town whose inhabitants are straight out of *Paris, Texas*.

There are three men outside the garage. They are the brothers, Mynhardt and Lucas van Schalkwyk and Mynhardt's friend Koos. Koos, Mynhardt tells the women a little later, is "not all there". Lucas spots his main chance to make some money and tells the women their car is irreparable. According to him they will have to wait until he can get a new engine from Queenstown, a city some distance away. This will take a day or two. He assures them there is no other alternative. He phones his friend Pieter in Queenstown to arrange for a new engine to be delivered in a day or so.

When the women find out that the only hotel burnt down two years ago and there is nowhere for them to stay, they are devastated. Especially when Koos tells them about "The Whistler", a creepy character who apparently scares women by whistling outside their bedrooms late at night when they are alone at home.

The ever-kind Mynhardt asks Lucas if the women can stay at their house. Lucas agrees reluctantly. The women, Koos and Mynhardt take their bags to the house. It is filthy: cigarette posters "from the sales reps" stuck on the wall, newspapers piled up everywhere, kittens splashing in milk under the kitchen table and new-born puppies in the bathroom. Sarah is disgusted but Cassie is too polite to show any disdain.

Mynhardt is fascinated by Cassie, which upsets Sarah. Sarah decides she needs a lot of alcohol to get her through the night. Especially when Cassie seems less than delighted with

Sarah's sexual overtures when they discuss sharing a bed in the spare room.

They go to the only shop in the town where cat food and KY Jelly share shelf space. Poppie runs the shop. She is not happy with these women coming into town. She treats them with deep suspicion. Sarah buys up all the supplies of liqueur, almost past its sell-by date, and as much brandy as she can afford.

They return to the house laden with alcohol. Lucas returns, and they are soon joined by the local traffic cop, Frans, Poppie's husband. He is keen to show off in front of the new ladies in his town. As there is nothing else to do, all of them drink steadily.

Sarah becomes drunker and also more jealous of Cassie by the minute, especially as Cassie seems quite taken with the gentle Mynhardt. Sarah initiates a game of Truth and Consequences to alleviate her boredom. Seething quietly, Sarah elicits Lucas' ill nature to side with her in her bitter attack on Mynhardt and Cassie and anyone who gets in her way in the vicious game.

Sarah's sharp intelligence quickly senses deep tension between the two brothers. She is relentless in her probing questions and soon unearths a dark secret the brothers have kept hidden for years: Marta, a young black girl Mynhardt had loved deeply, had been raped by Lucas. She died giving birth to Koos, and the oxygen-deprived baby was brought up by Poppie. Koos is either Lucas' or Mynhardt's child.

Excited, jealous, drunk and angry at Cassie and Mynhardt, Sarah loses it completely and goads Mynhardt into taking his revenge on his brother for the terrible thing he'd done to Marta years before. In a fit of rage, Mynhardt kills Lucas.

As the sobering reality sets in Sarah falls apart. Poppie arrives to fetch Frans, and finds Lucas's body instead. Never one to flinch from a crisis, especially as she's a butcher's daughter, Poppie decides to solve the problem in the way she knows best. She sends the two hysterical women to the bedroom and calls on the men to help her remove the evidence.

In the morning, there are too many bin bags lining the pavement. The sun is getting hot. The bin men are on strike and the dogs are beginning to gather ... The truth will out. It is only a matter of time ...

And that is when Pieter arrives from Queenstown with the engine. He's come to see Lucas.

Ends

Treatment of *A Shot at the Big Time*

The Army's about to replace his guitar with a gun ...

A small-town rock star faces a big-time future, but the army's about to replace his guitar with a gun.

Jimmy's family has personal crises instead of family holidays, but he finds his soul in his music. Until the army sends him his call-up papers. He has to choose between following the rules or following his heart. He decides to sing his own tune. He steals a rifle and goes AWOL. Back home he gives the performance of his life, alternating guitar riffs with rapid rifle fire. Until he hears the sound no musician wants to hear: the cries of a dying woman. It seems the army will take its pound of flesh. Even if it costs him his life. Petrus is a township boy whose family is trapped in the poverty of apartheid. Petrus' friendship with Jimmy opens his eyes to a potentially better life, one which has music and lyrics. He plays with the band whenever the authorities aren't looking and dreams of the big time. But this freak accident makes him decide there is only one future possible: he chooses to fight for freedom against white men. Men like his former friend, Jimmy.

Statement of Intent

A Shot at the Big Time is based on the true story of my brother in particular, and about the futility of war in general. I have used my brother's story, which is Oedipal in its tragic intensity, to focus on the senselessness of the South African Defence Force's (SADF) conscription campaign during the seventies and eighties in this country. This film will include in its compass the experience of one soldier in uMkhonto weSizwe (MK), the military wing of the ANC. It is an anti-war film in the classic tradition of *Apocalypse Now, Platoon, Born on the Fourth of July, M.A.S.H.* and *Catch 22*, among others. It is also a tirade against cruel authority and fundamentalism. For this reason, *One Flew Over the Cuckoo's Nest* was also an inspiration when writing this script.

The only thing Jimmy, my brother, didn't want to do was to kill another human being. The terrible irony is that by trying to defy the army and its constrictions, he broke the rules and went AWOL, taking a rifle with him to give the finger to the forces in the way he thought best. Through a series of random coincidences, an innocent homeless woman was killed by a ricochet bullet from his rifle when he and his friends were firing into the local rubbish dump. This event was too much for him to bear and he had a mental breakdown. He was put into a mental institution for months. But it didn't take long for the army to reclassify him as fit to serve on the border. When he was sent to the border, a staff sergeant forced him to engage in active combat against his will. Three days after his arrival, he was dead. Official reports said he was killed by a ricochet bullet. I believe, and people who were on the border with him at that time told me, that he shot himself rather than engage in active combat.

I would like to tell his story and that of all those young men who went to fight a war some of them weren't committed to. Some of them, like my brother, were only 17 when they were called up. South African men are still suffering severely as a result of what they went through in conscripted service. Everyone I've spoken to, who has been through this war, has urged me to tell this story.

Character Biographies

Jimmy: a white 17-year-old boy from a dysfunctional home. Father is an alcoholic with an aversion to paying bills and they move from pillar to post, always just one step ahead of the debt collectors. Jimmy seeks refuge from the lack of positive role models in his harsh life by immersing himself in his music. He is a gifted guitarist and wants to be a rock star until he is conscripted to the army. His hatred of the army is compounded by the brutal treatment he receives from one of the officers in command. The only problem is that the army holds all the aces.

Jess: white. Jimmy's adoring younger sister (15) who bears witness to the events.

Jimmy's father, Frank: white. A well-meaning alcoholic (40-something) who can't support his family although he always means to do better. He takes his frustrations out on Jimmy, by beating him and anyone else who gets in his way.

Jimmy's mother, Mary: white. A woman (early forties) who is overwhelmed by her circumstances. She doesn't have the self-esteem or the power to change the circumstances around her, even when she needs to help her son the most. Her children are everything to her and she loves her son, Jimmy, especially. She watches helplessly as he is brutalised by first his father, then the army.

Petrus: a 17-year-old black man who grew up with Jimmy. He spends time with Jimmy and the band whenever he can escape the watchful eyes of the apartheid system. He teaches Jimmy to play the guitar when they are both young. Initially, they have only their love of guitar-playing in common, but they soon discover they both have alcoholic fathers. And both have a deep passion for music that supersedes everything else in their lives. When Jimmy is forced to join the army and the tragic accident happens where Petrus' sister is killed, he takes his indigenous name, Vuyo, and decides to join MK. Jimmy's story in the SADF parallels Vuyo's experiences in uMkhonto weSizwe.

Band member, Gio: (20) a young white man who has avoided the army through having Italian citizenship and having wealthy parents. He sticks by Jimmy until the girl is killed. Then he and the other band members abandon him.

Band member, Rocky: white. A childhood friend of Jimmy's and Jess', and now a member of the band.

Band member, Sam: white. A friend of Jimmy's and a somewhat loose cannon. He is also a member of the band. He is a happy-go lucky boy from a fairly ordinary background who joins the band for the fame and the girls.

Neliswa: a young black woman. Petrus/Vuyo's sister (16) who has a crush on Jimmy and tries to watch the band play during their alternative concert on the rubbish dump. It is her unfortunate fate to be in the wrong place at the wrong time.

Wiese: white. A corporal in the army (thirties) who is takes an instant dislike to Jimmy because he is English-speaking and because he is a musician. He soon makes it his life's work to terrorise Jimmy, especially when Van Staden seems to take Jimmy under his protective wing.

Van Staden: white. A commanding officer (forties/fifties) in the camp where Jimmy is sent to do his basic training. Initially he likes Jimmy very much when he discovers Jimmy is a musician. He sets out to befriend him. He is a sensitive man trapped in an unhappy marriage, but he soon shows Jimmy he wants more than friendship. Jimmy has to decide whether Van Staden's price for an easy ride through the army is worth paying. But when Jimmy doesn't succumb to Van Staden's seduction, Van Staden makes him pay the ultimate price for being a rebel.

Martins: white. A kindred spirit in the army who befriends Jimmy in the barracks. Both are of English descent and are branded "Souties" – salt dicks – with one foot in England and the other in South Africa. So they stick together to try to find some sort of sanity in the army.

Gerhard: white. A traditional Afrikaner Nationalist who comes to the army to do the right thing and follow orders. However, even he finds that the army has no logic and he is side-lined by his own "volk". He finds that the Englishmen or "Souties" are far more to his liking than he'd first thought.

Synopsis

Jimmy is a rock star and his groupies are mad about him. All 13 of them. That's because Jimmy plays lead guitar for *The O.D. Boys,* a group of rock star wannabes in the Free State town of Odendaalsrus.

Petrus, the township boy who gets drafted in as the band's roadie, cements a friendship with Jimmy as they share shattered lives and strong joints. Petrus taught Jimmy to make a guitar out of an old oil tin when they were both small boys. Their dreams grow with their skills. Petrus hopes that maybe he too can become a rock star. And when the authorities aren't looking, Petrus picks up the guitar and plays with the band too.

An agent from the big city hears the band play and Jimmy's world blasts into orbit. With a record deal (and some anonymous love letters) in his top pocket, Jimmy's about to hit the Big Time. Until the postman brings him his army call-up papers.

And so he starts the jail sentence that is National Service in the South African Defence Force. A corporal called Wiese has a bullet with Jimmy's name on it. He sets out to break his spirit. With the brutal training in the fine art of killing, Jimmy finds that his sensitive soul is getting de-tuned.

Until a commanding officer called Van Staden seems set to rescue Jimmy from Wiese's ways. Van Staden is a fellow musician and feels an affinity for Jimmy's sensitive spirit. He takes him under his wing, driving Wiese into an even more impotent fury.

However, there is no such thing as a free lunch, and Van Staden soon lets Jimmy know the price he has to pay for his protection. Van Staden wants a little more than platonic friendship. Jimmy is shocked. He tries to let Van Staden down gently. But hell has no fury as a commanding officer scorned. It is only a matter of time before Van Staden takes away Jimmy's guitar and his first weekend pass, the one which would have seen him cutting his first record track with the record company.

So Jimmy breaks the rules. All of them. The worst of them. He goes AWOL but not before he has stolen back his guitar, and – to show Van Staden what he really thinks of him and the army – an R1 rifle with many rounds of ammunition.

When Jimmy gets back to Odendaalsrus, he hears that the recording session has been cancelled. He almost loses heart. He decides to play anyway. Alternating guitar riffs with rapid rifle fire, he and his fellow band members stage an impromptu concert at the local rubbish dump. They give the performance of their lives.

Petrus hears that Jimmy is back, and he and his sister, Neliswa, the author of the pink love letters, decide to watch him play. Neliswa shyly hides behind the rubbish dump to watch as Petrus hops up on stage to accompany the band with his tin guitar.

Suddenly a scream is heard. One of the bullets ricocheted off an old fridge and punctured the heart of Neliswa. In panic, the rest of the band members flee, leaving Jimmy to face the music of Petrus's grief alone. That is when Jimmy learns that Neliswa is the author of his love letters and Petrus decides that his father is right after all: all whites are his enemy.

The back-up vocalist, Sam, runs to the cops and sings like a canary. When Jimmy realises what he has done, he has a mental breakdown. He is arrested by the military police and Van Staden chooses to throw him into "The Nutcracker Suite", the psychiatric unit dedicated to getting shell-shocked soldiers back into action. Whether they like it or not.

When Jimmy is finally discharged from active duty, nobody wants to know him anymore. Worse than that, he can't seem to get the music to flow from his fingers again.

Meanwhile, Petrus has changed his name to Vuyo and joined uMkhonto weSizwe (MK), determined to fight for his freedom against all the racist whites.

That is when Jimmy gets "re-volunteered" by Van Staden to be one of an elite squad of trained maniacs who will go on search-and-destroy missions on the Angolan border. Even though he pleads and begs, his bags are packed for him, and he is waved off at the station by his parents and his last remaining fan, his sister.

Against his will, Jimmy is forced to go on a mission into enemy territory by a malicious sergeant major. Jimmy jumps out of the Bedford truck with the rest of the soldiers, but instead of firing at will, he releases the magazine with all the bullets from his rifle. As he walks out into the veld on his own, with enemy fire ringing around his ears, he strums his rifle as if it is a guitar. He walks straight towards a group of MK cadres.

Before Jimmy sees them, Vuyo recognises his old friend. He tells his comrades to hold their fire. For a long, long moment, he stares at Jimmy, his rifle pointed towards his heart. Then Jimmy sees his friend in the bushes and is broken at the sight of him. He drops to his knees and begs him to shoot him. Vuyo hesitates, about to walk towards Jimmy who is still begging to be shot when one of the other cadres shoots a hail of bullets deliberately into Jimmy's body. Vuyo is furious. He grabs the dying Jimmy, who thanks him for putting an end to it all. As Jimmy dies in his arms, the only thing that matters to either of them is their childhood friendship.

Van Staden phones Jimmy's family to tell them their son and brother has been killed by a ricochet bullet. Their lives are changed forever.

Ends

TASK

Write the best treatment you can!

Recommended reading

Friedmann, Julian, *How to Make Money Scriptwriting*. Intellect, 2000.

CHAPTER 6

FINDING THE BEAT

What is a beat sheet? How do you write an effective beat sheet? This chapter focuses on how writing a good beat sheet enables a writer to create a useful step outline, which forms the bones of the script itself.

1. What is a Beat Sheet?

A beat sheet is a list of story events – a list of what happens in the story in as succinct a way as possible. It's essentially a list of the action of a film and a description of exactly what the audience will see.

A beat sheet is kept as brief as possible. The evocative and carefully phrased writing of a pitch and a treatment is in stark contrast to a beat sheet. A beat sheet cuts the writing down to the bone. Brevity and accuracy are more essential here than flourishes of creative writing. Honing these skills now will prepare you for writing the script later.

One aspect of writing a beat sheet was especially difficult for me to grasp when I first started taking scriptwriting seriously. I was baffled by Robert McKee's assertion that "each beat should move the action forward in some meaningful way, and the value of the scene should change after each series of beats". In other words, a beat should never be in the beat sheet simply for the sake of exposition or telling of the story.

A beat should neither fill in a character's back story nor facilitate time lapses between scenes. A beat has to work towards affecting the character or story in a meaningful way.

This has remained one of the most difficult aspects of scriptwriting for me to master. When I first read Robert McKee's description that "every single beat of a film should work towards turning the value of a scene from positive to negative or negative to positive", I wrote: "Is he mad?" in the margin of the book. However, on re-reading his work more carefully, I realised that McKee was asserting that each beat must be meaningful enough to add up to significant change of value in a scene.

According to McKee, a beat should never remain static in value. There has to be a shift in the emotional value of every beat. The way to achieve this is to ensure that every beat contains vital information only and must never include story padding.

Essentially though, a beat sheet is a step-by-step breakdown of your story events in the way they will be seen in the final film. The events do not need to be explained in detail beyond what will be visible onscreen. The beat sheet is a roadmap of sorts to demarcate the journey your character takes through the world of your story.

Writing a beat sheet has become an essential scriptwriting tool for me. During the first five years of my career when I wandered alone in the scriptwriting wilderness, I would start a story at point A and then write towards whichever point my imagination took me. Sometimes the journey was worthwhile and I reached point Z, or thereabouts. Very often, though, I got horribly lost along the way.

I will not work on a commissioned film with a director or producer at this stage of my career unless we agree on a beat sheet before writing the full script. The reason for this is due to a few brutal experiences. These experiences taught me not to start writing a film or a project until the production team and I have **signed off** on the mutually agreed beat sheet. After working with two different producers and directors on *A Matter of Time* for over five years, where I rewrote the complete script so many times I lost count, I learnt that you can get so confused by trying to make sense of a director or producer's non-specific notes that you lose the authentic heart of your story. As a result, what you produce in the end is seldom a good script but most likely a very poor imitation of the original.

In fact, the act of rewriting a feature film script when you have just a few vague notes from a director or producer to work with is a sign of inexperience on both the part of the director as well as that of the writer. Don't ever agree to this. Insist on talking though and reworking the beat sheet until all of you agree to the story as a whole before you start what could become endless rewrites of a script. This will preserve your sanity. I say this only because I was driven to the point of a near breakdown after five years in the wilderness of development hell.

By the time I was given the commission to write *White Lion*, I had learnt my lesson well. I could see the potential pitfalls ahead in this project, as the production team consisted of an executive producer who had very definite ideas of what he wanted, a first-time producer, a first-time director, and a line producer who wanted a say in all the creative decisions. I insisted from the start that we worked on a beat sheet before starting the script. We spent three months fine-tuning the direction of the story using the beat sheet only. We then moved on to a step outline which is a more detailed version of the beat sheet, until we finally agreed on the direction of the script. To have rewritten the script every time one of the production team changed his mind would have been a nightmare.

2. Structuring Your Beat Sheet

To explain the basics of a beat sheet, it's a good idea to look at Robert McKee's excellent description of how to break down the structure of your script. I'll quote from his excellent book, *Story*.

Essentially, McKee describes structure as a selection of events from your main protagonist's life story "composed into a strategic sequence to arouse specific emotions and to express a specific view of life".

What this means is that your choice of the events which you are going to show the audience is as much a part of the story as is your choice of character or location. It's essential that you approach the structuring of your story with the same diligence and care that you used when conceiving your character and their broad journey. The old adage "the medium is the message" is never more apt than when dealing with scriptwriting. The way you tell your story is informed by your choice of film events and this is what sets an exceptional scriptwriter apart.

One of my favourite films, *American Beauty* (1999), is an excellent example of this. The seemingly random act of rose-cutting chosen by screenwriter, Alan Ball, to introduce the character of Carolyn Burnham is not a random choice. It's only the fourth scene of the film and takes place on page three of the script. We've already heard a voiceover from Lester Burnham telling us that "jerking off in the shower ... is the high point of my day". His voiceover has also told us that he will be dead "by the end of the year" and "in a way I'm dead already". We know that his life is far from perfect.

In contrast to Lester's words, the scene introducing Carolyn begins with a close-up on a rose which is called an American Beauty. It's a perfect rose. This rose isn't called an American Beauty by chance. It's a very deliberate choice by the screenwriter.

Readers of the script will be alerted immediately to the rose having the same name as the title of the film. People watching the film, however, unless they are rose enthusiasts, might not be aware that the rose is named thus.

Next Carolyn's gloved hands come into the shot and snip the rose off its perfect stem. She is then revealed to the audience at last as "a very well put together woman of 40 (who) wears colour co-ordinated gardening togs and has lots of useful and expensive tools".

She proceeds to have a conversation with the neighbours, a gay couple both called Jim. The fact that they are both called Jim is also no laziness on the part of the writer. You can draw your own conclusions as to why he calls them both Jim. I have my own, which are to do with the way the "gay neighbours" are put in a generic category as a couple. They reflect Carolyn's categorisation of them as the ubiquitous gay neighbours and her forcefully false acceptance of their alternative lifestyle is designed to be an outward show to the world of how broadminded she is.

Carolyn is effusive, praising Jim #1's tie excessively. He asks her what she does to make her roses flourish so well. Carolyn answers that she puts "eggshells and Miracle Grow" on her roses. Once again this is not a chance remark.

Roses are used extensively as the symbol of the ideal American Dream life throughout the film. This myth of the American Dream has been perpetuated especially since the Second World War. John F Kennedy epitomised this lifestyle, with his handsome ways and "perfect" wife and family. Americans were told that they deserve to have it all. In fact, this idea is enshrined in their constitution, which states that anyone has the right to succeed in the wonderful USA and everyone is entitled to happiness. The roses, especially in the fantasy scenes when Lester visualises a relationship with his daughter's friend, Angela, are the embodiment of this promise.

Each time Lester has his fantasy about Angela, rose petals rain down on him until he and the imagined Angela are covered in them.

Eggshells, on the other hand, symbolise brittleness. "Miracle Grow" is an artificial fertiliser, chemically designed to encourage growth without giving regard to any long-term damage it might inflict on the environment. With her own brand of forced artificial cheerfulness – the eggshells on which her family are forced to walk – and the fake fertiliser of enforcing the "perfect" home and garden on her family, Carolyn is trying to nurture her vision of having the ultimate American Dream. She nips in the bud the lives of her husband and daughter whenever they dare to flower independently of her. Think of the scene later in the film where Lester breaks out of his good-husband mould and drinks beer in the lounge in the middle of the day. For a moment, he almost gets through to Carolyn. They are about to make love on the sofa when she realises that he has spilled a little beer on the sofa. Immediately she is more concerned about the state of the furnishings than she is about their relationship. Her concern about appearances destroys a potential moment of reconciliation.

Allan Ball has cleverly conveyed all that is to come in those few opening beats with Carolyn. He has set her up as someone determined to fit into a mould of her imagined ideal family. And that means that everything in her life is for display purposes only.

All aspects of the above short scene work together to create the impression that Carolyn is concerned only about superficialities and the scene also initiates the symbolism of the rose, which winds its way throughout the film.

Ball's brilliant choice of subtle but definite action and dialogue evokes so much more than a mere progression of the storyline. The short scene creates thematic resonances to which audiences will relate whether they are aware of them or not.

It's a perfect example of a selection of events from your main protagonist's life story "composed into a strategic sequence to arouse specific emotions and to express a specific view of life", as McKee expresses it. It is no wonder that this film won five Oscars, one of them of course, for the screenwriter. This is the type of writing all of us should strive for and if we are lucky, we may achieve it at times.

Once again, if we examine the scene above, it is structured in such a way that it defines Carolyn's character as well as giving us the setting of the story.

The **sequence of events** creates the scene. Each event in the above scene is known as a **beat**. Remember that ideally each beat has to create a change in the storyline and/or character. Beats are supposed to affect the story in a meaningful way.

McKee explains that a beat should "create meaningful change in the life situation of a character that is expressed and experienced in terms of a value". He adds: "Values are the soul of storytelling. Ours is the art of expressing to the world a perception of values … Story values are the universal qualities of human experiences that may shift from positive to negative, from one moment to the next".

So we can see in the first two beats of Carolyn's scene, the rose is cut down in its prime. We also see that her ensemble ensures that she is designer chic at all times. Her desire for perfection is evident. If we had to assign a value to these two beats, I'd say that they were from Honesty to Deception.

The broad assignation of such a strong value to this beat is a bit of a push at this stage and is informed by what I know is to come in the rest of the film. So perhaps a more conservative value could be assigned here as the battle between the values of Integrity versus Superficiality. Perhaps we should leave it at that for now.

3. Finding the Beat

Let us examine the above scene. Remember, in the beat sheet, you have to think visually at all times.

The first objects we see are the rose, and then Carolyn's gloved hands cutting the rose off its stem. There are two small events here in the single beat. In the beat sheet it would read as follows:

```
An American Beauty rose is cut off at its stem
by designer-gloved hands.
```

The first meaningful event is subtle: the rose is cut down. Its symbolism becomes apparent only as the film unfolds. The extended metaphor of roses and rose petals reinforces the idea of roses as a symbol of the American Dream. In the beat sheet, however, the decimation of the rose is an important event as the writer is aware of what roses symbolise, even though the audience might not be. Yet.

The next beat will read as follows:

```
The hands belong to Carolyn, whose designer
gardening gloves match her clogs and shears.
```

Once again, the matching outfit tells us about Carolyn, her need to wear a designer outfit at all times, even while gardening. We learn a great deal about Carolyn and her values in both these beats.

The next beat should read like this:

```
Gay neighbour, Jim #1, comes out to tell his
dog to stop barking as the dog has just had
a walk.
```

Lester's voiceover tells us that both members of the gay couple next door are named Jim. The subtle message is that they are not individuals, but a ubiquitous gay couple who are there to reflect how "enlightened" Carolyn thinks she is by her apparently accepting attitude towards them.

The dog is chastised for barking. In Jim #1's mind, and Carolyn would agree with him, dogs are meant to be seen and not heard. They are decorative accessories to show that even a gay couple can be a family with a dog in lieu of a child. Heaven forbid that the dog behaves like a dog.

The next beat should read like this:

```
Carolyn compliments Jim#1 effusively on his tie.
He asks Carolyn what she uses to make her roses
flourish. She tells him, "Eggshells and Miracle
Grow."
```

This conversation qualifies as a beat as the words spoken by Carolyn add to the impact of her superficiality. The significance of the eggshells and Miracle Grow has already been explained.

The next beat is created by a voiceover.

```
Voiceover: Lester says he gets exhausted
watching his wife. She wasn't always like this,
he says. They used to be happy.
```

Now you might think that this voiceover is exposition, just filling in the back story and so on. I believe, however, that the juxtaposition of the visual of Carolyn's falsely bright conversation with her trendy neighbours with Lester's voiceover, full of world-weary cynicism, undercuts Carolyn's façade and exposes it for what it is.

This juxtaposition of the visual with the contradiction of the voiceover changes the value of the scene enormously. The audience learns what they might have suspected already: all is not well in this home. Remember the tag line of the film? It is "Look Closer". In these early scenes we are already being encouraged not to buy into Carolyn's version of what the Burnham household is like.

In McKee's words, the scene "turns" from one value to another. The false brightness of Carolyn's world is shown to be a sham by her husband's cynical comments. As the authorial narrator in this film, we know Lester's version of the truth is the one to be trusted.

That is the end of the brief but very profound scene. Put together the beat sheet would look like this:

American Beauty Beat Sheet of Scene Four

```
An American Beauty rose is cut off at its stem by
designer-gloved hands.

The hands belong to Carolyn, whose designer
gardening gloves match her clogs and shears.

Gay neighbour, Jim #1, comes out to tell his dog
to stop barking as the dog has just had a walk.
(His partner joins him).

Carolyn compliments Jim #1 effusively on his
tie. He asks Carolyn what she uses to make her
roses flourish. She tells him, "Eggshells and
Miracle Grow."

Voiceover: Lester says he gets exhausted
watching his wife. She wasn't always like this,
he says. They used to be happy.

End Scene Four.
```

Do you notice that the many notes I made about the significance of each beat are not mentioned in the beat sheet? However, the screenwriter's selection of specific events to depict on screen are extremely well thought out and work together to enforce the larger themes of the film. Allan Ball has worked long and hard to choose these precise and profound beats to create this short scene. This is your task in this chapter.

I will modify a phrase from a friend, David Nicoll, who describes poetry using this metaphor instead of film. If the film is the pot of soup, the beat sheet is the Oxo stock cube which provides the rich flavour.

4. The Beat Creates the Whole

As I said earlier, your focus in this section is not on writing beautiful lines, as you did in your pitch and treatment. The focus and intensity must be directed at the **selection of the events** or **beats** you decide to show the audience. As you can see from Allan Ball's scene above, his choice of visual moments is very well thought out. Each beat carries a profound message about the characters and their world in *American Beauty*.

This is the same intensity you must bring to your work on the beat sheet. The energy you expend on this section will ensure that when it comes to writing the script you will be more than ready for it and will have much less work to do.

Writing the beat sheet also means that you must revisit Chapter 1, and look at your hero's journey again. A beat sheet and screenplay structure work alongside each other. You have to structure your beat sheet into the best three-act screenplay you can, using the blueprint of the hero's journey as your guide.

McKee explains that each series of beats creates a sequence, or a scene, as you saw above with Scene Four from *American Beauty*. He does give us a little leeway in saying that even if every single beat does not change value itself, at least the beats should work towards every scene changing its value from positive to negative or vice versa. For screenwriters who aren't quite of the calibre of Allan Ball, this is a welcome relief.

So every beat builds up a sequence; sequences create a scene; a series of scenes climaxes in an act; each act's climax builds up towards the final climax in the final act, which concludes the screenplay.

Once again, briefly: **beats** lead to a **sequence**, which create a **scene**, and the scenes create an **act**. The acts create a **screenplay**.

Structure your beat sheet in such a way that you will be creating the **climax** or **turning points** at exactly the right moments of each act, using the hero's journey blueprint from Chapter 1. It is well worth putting in much effort into this stage of the process as it is one of the most difficult steps. If you do it well, your beat sheet is able to be expanded just a little more to create the **step outline**. This step outline can then be elaborated on a little more to create your script.

Let me give you an example from my work. This is one of the earliest drafts of the beat sheet for the feature film *White Lion*. The final product has come a long way since this first beat sheet. But it shows where we started. Remember that the production team and I worked on the script just using beat sheets for over three months. You will see that I kept an awareness of the hero's journey in my head as the production team didn't know about this being the reasoning behind my script at this stage of the procedure. I labelled the acts too, for my own sense of clarity. Remember, this was a simple first draft beat sheet. It changed a great deal through the development process.

Beat Sheet *White Lion* First Draft

```
                    ACT 1

(Birth to three months)

Heavily pregnant Mala (lioness) takes herself
off to the thicket.

Mala gives birth - one tawny and one white cub.
She licks them upside down. Aahh!

Mala forced to go hunting, leaves cubs alone.

White cub ventures out; tawny brother follows.

White cub attracts attention of passing hyena.
Hyena kills cub. Bloodied body in jaws. Which
one is it?

Tawny cub is dead. White cub distressed.
```

Hyena about to go after white cub, Letsatsi, but Mala comes back in time.

Mala chases off hyena.

Mala sees blood smears: remains of tawny cub. It's not safe to be out with Letsatsi. His white coat attracts predators. It's time to go back to the pride.

Mala introduces Letsatsi to the pride. Temba, the pride male, likes him. Bravo, another male lion, hates him.

Letsatsi tries to join in with cub games. He is rejected.

Bravo initiates the constant "walk away" from the white cub with the other lions at different times.

Nearby a rifle shot is fired in veld. In the pride Mala reacts, ears pricking up.

Nearby, a dead lion hits the ground. Two professional hunters, happy, lift up the dead lion's head, delighted with their kill.

ACT 2

(Eight months - ten months).

Lions are hunting buffalo in the veld. Big confusion - dust, blood, the pulse of muscular bodies bearing down on their kill.

Letsatsi on outskirts of the kill, watching.

Aftermath. Dead beast on ground. Temba goes for his usual lion's share of the kill. Bravo pushes him away. It is time for the takeover.

Big confrontation between Bravo and Temba. Temba driven out of the pride.

In aftermath of the coup, Letsatsi is ousted by Bravo in vicious fight.

Bravo snarls at Mala to make her realise he is king of the castle now. Mala submits helplessly.

Wounded, Letsatsi is alone far from the pride. It rains heavily. Bedraggled, this young lion's future looks bleak. He watches the blood streaming off his leg in the rain.

Days have passed. Letsatsi's ribs are showing. Wound has dried in hard, caked blood.

The hyena is trailing Letsatsi, sensing the white lion's weakness. He is prepared to bide his time to wait for an easy kill.

Letsatsi's hunting attempts are futile. Prey escapes easily in a couple of scenes: tries to eat tortoise; porcupine. Letsatsi isn't doing well.

The hyena makes his first attempt on Letsatsi.

Letsatsi just manages to fight him off.

Fat American has come to Africa to bag his kill; arrives at local farmhouse to stay overnight with professional hunter (PH).

Farmer welcomes him. PH is his son.

Hungry Letsatsi sees another teenage tawny lion, Bongani, about to scavenge an impala carcass at the edge of the riverbed.

Hyena is still trailing Letsatsi.

Letsatsi watches Bongani at the river from a distance. Sees a crocodile's eyes peeping out of river near the carcass, waiting to pounce.

Just in time, Letsatsi pushes the tawny lion aside, out of harm's way, as the crocodile rears out of water snapping shut on fresh air rather than tawny lion.

Letsatsi has saved Bongani. Bongani licks Letsatsi's crusted wound clean.

Bongani makes easy buck kill, and allows Letsatsi to share it.

Friendship cemented, the teenagers run riot on the veld: encounter warthog/giraffe/elephant: fun scenes.

Bongani and Letsatsi fancy chicken takeaways from farmhouse and raid farmer's coop for fresh chicken, killing more than they eat.

Farmer runs out screaming when his dog alerts him to the raid.

Visiting fat American comes out and sees the white lion. He's intrigued.

Farmer fires shots. Misses.

Lions hightail it out of there.

Fat American tells the hunter and the PH that he wants the white lion.

Letsatsi and Bongani, covered in chicken feathers, sleep as the sun rises, tummies full.

At sunrise, the hunters are loading up rifles, tents onto Land Rover to bag themselves a lion.

PH and American drive away from farmhouse for their official hunt. Farmer wishes them luck.

Letsatsi and Bongani still fast asleep.

Shots go off.

A lion is dead. Which one is it? It is the tawny lion. Fat American is a terrible shot.

Bongani is motionless, covered in blood.

Letsatsi runs away in a hail of ineffectual bullets.

Fat American furious. He wants that white lion.

Letsatsi is alone again. (Again because of his colour his second "brother" has been killed.) He hangs his head, defeated, but only for a moment.

The hunters are camping overnight. Bongani's body is draped over the Landie.

Letsatsi watches until the men are in the tents.

When the only light remaining is the firelight, he makes his way down to the camp.

He picks his way through the cooking utensils, licking the braai grid, eating leftover boerewors.

He sniffs outside one side of the tent. No, that's not what he is looking for.

The other side. Yes. This is what he wants. He rips into the side of the tent, tearing the canvas as if it's cheap cotton.

The fat American is lying in his sleeping bag, white with terror as the angry lion is inches from his face.

Letsatsi roars. He slashes at the man with crazed paws.

The PH fumbles for his rifle.

Letsatsi swats the American who collapses back in a pathetic heap.

Before the PH can load, Letsatsi is gone.

The American is a gibbering wreck. And his sleeping bag looks suspiciously wet.

ACT 3

Time has passed.

Fully grown Letsatsi roams the plains alone.

He watches from a distance as another pride moves near him.

A large tawny male is in charge of the pride. Letsatsi looks down on them enviously.

The fat American is back! He tells the PH he is going to put that white lion to death once and for all.

Letsatsi is making a bid to take over the tawny male's pride. At the showdown between the two males, the hunters arrive.

In flurry of excitement, the two lions turn on the fat American.

Shots are fired.

Dust. Blood. Confusion. More dust. Stunned silence. Who is dead? Who is wounded? Nothing is clear.

The dust clears. On the ground is the large, tawny lion. Dead.

The fat American is being driven away to the airport by the PH.

The fat American's face is covered with bandages, his arm is badly wounded, and heavily strapped to his body. The PH tells him that he is lucky he is alive and he should count his lucky stars.

```
At sunset, a large male lion is silhouetted
against the glowering sky.

A female approaches and rolls submissively in
front of him.

She is joined by two other females and a few
playful cubs.

Only one of them is white.

Close-up of Letsatsi as his sapphire eyes survey
his territory.

He roars (in recognition and contentment) as his
pride gathers around him. The white cub plays
with the tuft of his tail.
```

Ends

This was the blueprint we started working on and progressed much further than this simple storyline. If you get the chance to see the film, you will realise how much has changed. There are many things which have not changed, however, and the broad structure has remained the same to some extent.

Notice, however, that explicit story details are left out except when absolutely necessary. Broad strokes are required when writing the beat sheet.

Now let's examine how a good beat sheet can lead to very useful step outline.

5. The Beat Creates the Step

As I mentioned before, a well-constructed beat sheet needs to be expanded with just a few more details to produce a good **step outline**. Sometimes a producer or director will ask you to produce a step outline so that they can get a better idea about the details of the storyline. This is not hard to do when you have written a well-thought-out beat sheet.

Once again, I'll give you examples of how the above beat sheets were expanded into step outlines. The first one is just the opening section from *White Lion*, which we had worked on for over a month already. You will see that I had added **scene headings** at this stage. This was also for my own sense of clarification. A step outline doesn't always have to have scene headings, but it does help to visualise your story.

Step Outline: *White Lion*

```
                      ACT 1

EXT - DAY. SAVANNAH - THICKET

A heavily pregnant tawny lioness, Mala, explores
a thicket near her pride's lair. She finds a
secluded grassy patch just far enough away
from the pride to deliver her cubs safely.
She flattens the grass with her large body in
preparation for the birth of her cubs.

EXT - DAY. MALA'S LAIR

(New-born Letsatsi)

Mala has given birth to two cubs. Their fur is
still wet from the birth and their eyes are
closed. One of the cubs is tawny like the rest
of the pride. The other is as white as fresh
milk. Mala licks them upside down in her attempt
to clean off the birth fluids. The cubs mew in
response to the touch of their mother's rasping
tongue. Instinct kicks in as they blindly root
for their mother's milk for comfort. Mala makes
throaty growls of contentment as she cleans her
newly born babies.

Late afternoon. A hyena yaps nearby. An exhausted
Mala raises her head. She is restless. The place
where her cubs are sheltered isn't safe anymore.
She will have to move them.

Mala carries one cub at a time to a new lair
nearby. The cub's legs dangle in the air as she
```

holds one softly in her mouth. She gently places the cub in the new thicket and then returns to fetch the next. Once she has them both safely in the new lair, she settles her large body down carefully next to her babies. The disturbed cubs are reassured now that they feel their mother's warmth next to them. They each find a teat and begin to suckle furiously, kneading her belly with small but insistent paws.

The cubs sleep blissfully next to their mother. Their bellies are round with milk, and Mala gazes out of her lair with heavy-lidded contentment. A steady purr from her furry depths transmits her sense of peace with the world.

EXT - DAY. MALA'S LAIR

Days have passed. The cubs' eyes have opened and they are doing well and becoming playful. Although Mala watches them like a hawk, she allows the cubs to move within the perimeter of their lair.

A brightly coloured butterfly illuminates the dry scrub around the cubs. They are entranced by this sight. Their heads move in unison as the butterfly flutters just out of their reach. The cubs squint as it hovers tantalizingly above their noses. As one, they decide to catch it. They paw the air, just missing the flighty butterfly every time. After a few too many false jabs, they cuff each other in frustration. The butterfly flutters away, leaving the two brothers involved in a battle of the paws.

The cubs are fascinated by the long, golden grass waving in the wind just outside their thicket. They watch the sweeping movements, entranced by the delicate swaying of the tufts of burnished grass. The cubs' heads move from side to side like spectators at a tennis match.

A fat dung beetle taps his way across the lair's floor. The cubs watch for a moment, intrigued by this small creature. Then they decide it's time to hunt. They trip over each other and their own paws in their enthusiasm to try and pin down the stoic beetle. Somehow, in spite of their efforts, the beetle continues to make its way across the lair's floor.

EXT - SUNSET. THE THICKET

Mala is very hungry. She has been feeding her cubs for weeks without eating anything herself. She has to venture out to get food or she will not produce any more milk.

Reluctantly she prepares to leave the thicket, looking back at her cubs before she goes. Reassured, as the cubs seem hidden in the lair she has made for them, she leaves.

EXT - NIGHT. THE THICKET

Moments pass silently. The cubs stay hidden until after Mala has gone. For a while they nuzzle into each other for warmth.

Then Letsatsi opens his eyes. He is bored. He nudges his brother awake. It is time for an adventure and he makes his way out of the lair. Sleepily, his tawny brother watches for a moment, and then follows cautiously behind Letsatsi.

The white cub's fur glows in the bright moonlight.

A passing hyena sees Letsatsi's white coat shining in the dark like a candle. Its eyes light up. Within a heartbeat, the hyena pounces.

The tawny cub panics and runs straight towards the hyena's dangerous jaws, as Letsatsi stands

frozen to the spot. There is a scuffle. The
hyena's jaws snap around the tawny cub. Shocked,
Letsatsi watches in horror as his brother
swings, limply dead, from the hyena's jaws.

The hyena turns towards Letsatsi.

It is about to attack when Mala returns to
the thicket. Just in time. She chases off
the hyena.

She sees the blood smears, and the remains of
her tawny cub.

She turns towards Letsatsi, licks him
protectively and picks him up in her strong
jaws. Mala carries him back into the depth of
the thicket.

Letsatsi has lost all of his bravado, and his
eyes flicker with fear. He nuzzles into her fur.

EXT - SUNRISE. THE THICKET

The lair isn't safe anymore. Mala leaves the
thicket with Letsatsi in her mouth. He is old
enough to introduce him to the pride.

EXT - DAY. TEMBA'S PRIDE

(8-10 weeks)

There is a rustle of interest as Mala walks back
into the pride. The lionesses resting in the
noonday sun watch her with hooded eyes as she
carries her cub in her mouth. She walks towards
Temba and puts the cub down next to him.

Letsatsi wobbles about for a moment as he
regains control of his feet.

The younger cubs in the pride look at him
with extreme interest. Here is something new
to feed their curiosity. A white lion cub has

never been seen before. While Mala settles herself near Temba to re-establish her place in the hierarchy, the younger lions circle the newcomer. A larger tawny male tries out his left hook on Letsatsi's head. The others follow suit. Soon, Letsatsi is being pushed about by the young cubs.

Mala gives a soft but commanding growl and the youngsters leave Letsatsi alone. He makes his way back to her for comfort and finds it safer to stay near her large body.

Temba's tail swishes lazily in front of Letsatsi's eyes. Letsatsi can't take his eye off the dark tuft of Temba's tail. He watches the tail with interest.

Temba ignores the cub completely. For now, he will simply tolerate this newcomer.

Letsatsi can't resist and he swats the big lion's tail with his little paw. Temba turns his head lazily and looks down at the white cub with some interest. He watches Letsatsi for a moment. Then looks away and yawns enormously.

Mala places a protective paw on Letsatsi. She will have to keep an eye on her cub in this pride.

Extract ends

You can see that it doesn't take much to elaborate on the beat sheet to create a more detailed step outline. What is important, though, is that you have to keep thinking visually. There can be no interior monologues unless you specify a voiceover.

You will also notice that the step outline has concertinaed the individual beats into larger scenes to make the story flow more easily. There is a little bit more room for personal expression at this stage of the process. You can decide whether to add scene headings or not.

If the producers specifically ask for scene headings, you obviously have to provide them.

I would suggest that the further along the line you are with the script, the more detail and description you add, including scene headings. The step outline for *White Lion* was close to the scripting stage, so I could include more script-like element such as scene headings.

You can decide whether to add critical lines of dialogue if you think they are essential to your step outline. **In essence, the step outline is an expansion of the beat sheet to add a little more flesh to the bones of the beat sheet.** It is also used to give a producer or a director a better sense of how the story will play out on the screen, so you can include details of set and the character's appearance.

TASKS

1. Bearing in mind all you have read above, **write the best beat sheet** you can for your script so far. Do not panic too much about getting it as perfectly written as Allan Ball's script, for example. This is just your first draft. You will be able to revise as much as is needed along the way. Do give it your best attention though. If you do this part of the planning process well, writing the script will be so much easier.
2. If you feel confident enough to **start working on a step outline**, go ahead and write it to the best of your abilities.

Chapter 7

WHAT DEFINES WRITING FOR FILM?

In this chapter I will examine the basics of scriptwriting technique, concentrating on format and style as well as the critical and careful use of dialogue. International conventions are used as the standard scriptwriting format.

1. Why is Writing for Film Different?

Scriptwriting technique differs hugely from writing prose or even stage plays. Because of the high cost of every second of screen time, the screenwriter has to be conscious of saying as much as possible with as few words as possible. The screenwriter must always be aware that they usually have no longer than an hour and a half to captivate an audience. In fact, if an audience isn't intrigued in the first few minutes, you will have to work very hard to earn their interest throughout the duration of the film. Remember, a good way to **hook** your audience in each scene is to "start late, finish early". In other words, the screenwriter has to **cut to the chase**.

I will use a few extracts from exceptional films to show how experienced screenwriters achieve this difficult task. I will also use a short film I wrote which attempted to encapsulate a big storyline in a short format.

2. How is Screenwriting Different?

Firstly, film scripts are written using a very specific format. For years I thought that trying to write a script according to a set format was a restriction on my creativity. I thought that any producer or director would be so entranced by my exquisite writing that they would see past the 300-odd pages of internal dialogue and long speeches and unearth the gem of a film which I was so sure that my script was. It took me a number of years and many, many rejections to realise that no producer or director worth their salt would look at my work unless it was formatted properly, just for starters.

Eventually, it was with a slightly resentful attitude that I began to listen to experts in the field. I realised that it was a fact that a director/producer would not read beyond the first page if the script was not in the correct **font** or if it was bound in the incorrect way. That knowledge explained the rejection of the many awfully written, but beautifully bound, scripts I'd submitted to producers by then.

However, scriptwriting technique is easy to learn. It's doesn't take much to learn how to format scene headings, character names, action statements, slug lines, dialogue and so on. What is less easy to learn is the **art** of screenwriting. After countless years of scriptwriting, I'm still learning to master this craft myself. However, I have come far enough along the path to be able to see that I'm much better than when I first started. Thankfully, my screenwriting is much more succinct now than those unworkable doorstoppers of the past. I still learn every day and know I'll continue to do that until I take my last breath. I hope you will approach scriptwriting in the same way: keep improving your craft with every single script.

3. What You See Is What You Get

Take a few hours to watch the opening minutes of one of your favourite films. Watch closely as you imagine what was written in the script to describe what you see on screen.

One Flew Over the Cuckoo's Nest

I'll use an example from one of my most loved films: *One Flew Over the Cuckoo's Nest*. This is a film based on the novel by Ken Kesey. The script was co-written by Lawrence Hauben and Bo Goldman and it was directed by Miloš Forman. Although it was made some time ago, it is still a masterpiece. Not only is it a superbly written and directed film, it is also one of the best performances by Jack Nicholson in his long and memorable career.

Interestingly enough, it was produced by Michael Douglas after his father, Kirk Douglas, had held the rights to produce the book for more than ten years. The story of how Kirk tried to produce *Cuckoo's Nest* ten years before it finally hit the screen is worthy of a whole chapter in itself. Suffice to say, Kirk Douglas had posted the book to his director of choice, Miloš Forman, in Poland after they'd met at a party in Hollywood and discussed turning Ken Kesey's novel into a film. Unknown to both of them, the parcel was stopped by the repressive Polish regime at their border post and never reached its destination. Kirk Douglas then spent the next ten years thinking what a rude bastard Forman was for not replying to him after sending him the book. At the same time Forman spent the next ten years thinking what a rude bastard Kirk Douglas was for never posting the book he'd promised. It took Michael Douglas, who finally decided to make use of the rights his father had held to the book for years, to unravel the misunderstanding. And that is how, ten years after a discussion in Hollywood with Kirk Douglas, Miloš Forman was called in by Michael Douglas to direct the film.

Michael Douglas produced the film and won the Best Picture Oscar for his very first production. *One Flew Over the Cuckoo's Nest* won five Academy Awards in total in 1975 and has been regarded as a classic ever since. If you can get hold of a copy of this film, do so. If not, just follow what I describe as I watched the opening scenes.

Scene description of *One Flew Over the Cuckoo's Nest*

The first shot of the film is a wide-screen long shot (LS) of a rural landscape. There are snowy mountain peaks in the distance and the foreground is filled with fields of grass. The landscape is fairly barren in spite of its beauty. The sun is rising over the mountains.

A single road snakes along the foot of the mountains. As the credits begin to roll, lights become visible at the left-hand corner of the screen. Unusual, slightly eerie music plays. The lights come closer and we become aware that it belongs to a car. The car's headlights move slowly along the road and across the screen, while the credits continue to flash onto the otherwise static screen. The only movement in the frame apart from the credits comes from the slow motion of the car in the distance with the lights slicing through the dawn. The car comes closer to the camera and the camera pans with it as it speeds alongside and then past the camera. The opening shot takes 1 minute and 17 seconds before it cuts to the next scene.

The next scene starts with a medium close-up (MCU) of an old, slack-jawed man lying in a grey hospital gown in a rumpled hospital bed. The camera pans from him to another patient in a bed alongside him, then past hospital cabinets alongside sleeping figures. One cabinet has a photo of a posing muscleman stuck onto it. The muscular, confident figure is in sharp contrast to the reclining man next to the cabinet. Another has a drawing of a Picasso-like painting of something similar to his *Guernica* stuck onto its side. The tortured figure in the drawing seems to be screaming.

Cut to the next scene.

A long, white corridor with a fence-like gate or grill at the end of it. A uniformed woman comes into the shot and walks briskly towards the camera and the gate. She has a black coat and hat on, which contrast starkly with the white surroundings. There is a red light above the gate. She unlocks the gate and walks through it, slamming it as she comes closer towards the camera. As she passes the camera the shot cuts to her back as she walks past three male orderlies mopping the gleaming white floor. They are dressed completely in white. They greet her – Miss Ratched – and she rattles her keys as she greets them and goes to unlock yet another door. They carry on mopping.

The camera cuts to the interior of the small room she is unlocking and we see her enter the room. Her black coat and hat are still in stark contrast to everything around her.

She locks the door behind her. Another nurse comes in with files. The younger nurse, dressed all in white, greets Miss Ratched briefly and goes towards the desk, carrying a file with her.

The next scene shows an apparently disturbed man behind bars as an orderly unlocks his cell. The orderly greets the man and unlocks his shackles as he asks him how he feels. The man mumbles that he feels rested.

The following scene shows the younger nurse laying out little cups with pills onto a tray. Each cup has a name next to it. She takes the tray to the counter behind a glass partition. Through the glass, we see the ward alongside filled with patients. The nurse approaches a microphone, which is on the counter, and her voice resounds into the general ward: "Medication time". She places a record on an old gramophone and it begins to play soothing but anodyne music.

The scene cuts between the ward side and the nurses' side of the glassed partition as the patients queue up, with the aid of orderlies, to receive their medication. The patients are docile, keen to take their medication while the soothing music plays. We see a number of odd-looking men in close-up as they take their pills. A large Native American man, Bromden, standing immobile while holding a broom, has to be prodded to move forward to take his medication.

Cut to the next scene.

Outside the hospital, the car we saw in the opening scene has drawn up to the elaborate portal of the institution. A guard/policeman opens the passenger door and urges someone to climb out of the car. The guard/policeman takes a small bag from the passenger, who finally emerges. The passenger has handcuffs on his wrists, a beanie on his head and wears jeans, a T-shirt, and a leather jacket.

The camera cuts to the point of view (POV) inside the institution's doors as we observe the man enter the large white doors. He is flanked by two uniformed guards/policemen as he comes towards the camera. A patient inside a barred door watches this new arrival with an inquisitive stare. The man in the beanie stares back at the patient with hooded eyes.

The man is now in a MCU shot with the guards alongside him. We get our first good look at the protagonist of this remarkable film: Randall P McMurphy. The guard hands over McMurphy's papers and bag to a nurse and the two orderlies from the previous scene. The nurse signs the form to take delivery of the man. The guard grabs McMurphy's wrists and unlocks the handcuffs, which are seen in a close-up (CU).

Deranged laughter is heard from somewhere upstairs and McMurphy looks up towards it. There is a large spiral staircase rising above. A number of odd-looking patients stare down at him with bemused looks. He glances up at them and smiles wryly. The guard frees his hands and the cuffs drop off. The guard puts away the keys and McMurphy stares at him for another moment. Then McMurphy laughs into the guard's face. He whoops like a monkey as he grabs one of the guards/policemen and kisses him roughly on the cheek.

We have met our main protagonist and we can see that he believes he already has the measure of the new place he is in.

The next scene cuts to the POV of the corridor with the caged door once more. The nurse, orderly and McMurphy are seen coming towards it. McMurphy laughs and dances as he nears the gate. A few patients straggle inside the gate as the nurse unlocks it. The soothing music is still playing. McMurphy is led through the gate by the orderlies. He sees the men lingering nearby. They ignore him completely and his face drops as he realises they have no idea who they are. He greets one of the men who does not respond at all. The nurse and orderlies go into the small office and tell Nurse Ratched that Mr McMurphy has arrived. Nurse Ratched has taken off her coat at last and is now dressed in her white uniform. McMurphy peers into the small nurses' room and has the door slammed in his face. Inside the office, Nurse Ratched continues stamping forms, then takes an inventory of the contents of the small bag McMurphy brought in.

It's six minutes into the film and we've met the protagonist, McMurphy, the antagonist, Nurse Ratched, and another of the most important characters in the film, Chief Bromden. No important dialogue has been spoken either. So far, the description I've given you above is visual storytelling at its best.

I wrote the above passages describing what I saw as I watched the film. How do you imagine you would transcribe the above into a script?

I searched the internet for the original script of *One Flew Over the Cuckoo's Nest*. It was a surprise to see how much the director changed the opening of the film from the original script, but the discrepancy is not that unusual. Directors often move away from the scriptwriter's initial written conception into filming a more pared-down, visual story, which is informed by the details contained in the writer's script.

I've included the first 14 pages, which covers almost the same ground as my description above of the first six minutes of the film. You can decide whether the director lost any vital elements leaving out so much detail from the original script. Also take note of how the format explains what we should see and hear in the film.

Extract begins

EXT. WORK FARM - NIGHTFALL

All we SEE is an ELEVATED SHOT of the distant mountains, rolling landscape and McMURPHY - one cheek laid-open and crusted over with dried blood, his face and prison work clothes caked with dried sweat and dust - as he sits on the very top of a water tower watching the last rays of sunlight.

A long moment passes before McMurphy's attention is drawn elsewhere and he looks down.

                REVERSE SHOT - McMURPHY'S POV

Far below, in the prison yard a MAN is SEEN hurrying across the yard where he joins a group of men composed of armed prison guards, officials, and medics - a stretcher, an ambulance, a fire truck and safety nets spread out at the base of the water tower. The man is seen talking to the officials, then a bullhorn is handed to him and they all look up at McMurphy.

                    McMURPHY

As he looks down at them, a searchlight is turned on him.

                    MAN (VO)
    (through bullhorn)
  McMurphy! This is Doctor Shankle, from the infirmary. Can you hear me?

McMurphy doesn't respond.

                  SHANKLE (VO)
    (through bullhorn)
  Can you hear me, McMurphy?

McMurphy doesn't respond. Another searchlight goes on as a SECOND VOICE is PICKED UP on the BULLHORN.

> SECOND VOICE
> (through bullhorn)
> Why don't we blast 'im, for Christ's sake, he ain't gonna come down ... you ...

The BULLHORN is TURNED OFF. A long moment passes as McMurphy continues to squat on the tower and wait. He shivers against the coming night when ...

> SHANKLE (VO)
> (through bullhorn)
> McMurphy!
> I have the warden's promise. If you come down, nobody will hurt you! You'll be in my custody! I promise!

An almost imperceptible smile appears on McMurphy's face.

INT. MEN'S DORM - OREGON STATE HOSPITAL - DAWN

Strange HUMMING SOUNDS, CLANKING PIPES and HISSING RADIATORS as we see beds, with patients lying asleep, line two walls. The third wall is a heavy-gauge steel grill, with a door that opens on to the day room. The door is open. On the far side of the day room, a long hallway with other doors opening into rooms: the latrine, washroom, tub room, mess hall, seclusion room, psychiatrist's office, visitors' room, etc.

Across the day room, a glass-enclosed nurses' station where TURKLE, a night attendant, is seen preparing to go off duty.

The CAMERA PANS the beds in the men's dorm. One man turns, another twists, a third lies as if dead.

CAMERA PAN ENDS on BROMDEN, who lies still, eyes wide open, very alert. He reaches down, plucks a stale piece of gum from under the bed frame, puts it in his mouth and starts chewing.

A beat, then Bromden carefully undoes the leather strap which binds him to the bed. He slips out of bed and quietly makes his way down the aisle, paying no attention to the other patients, some of whom are beginning to stir awake.

Ahead, at the end of the hallway, the door opens and three day attendants, WASHINGTON, WARREN and MILLER, dressed in white uniforms, enter and move down the hallway and disappear into a side room.

Bromden continues his silent journey towards the day room as Turkle emerges from the side door to the nurses' lounge, goes up the hallway as MISS PILBOW, the day nurse, comes in, passing Turkle on the way out. She crosses to the nurses' station and enters as Bromden reaches the day room.

INT. DAY ROOM - DAY

As Bromden makes his way across the day room, past the nurses' station, unnoticed by Miss Pilbow, who is busy preparing the day's medication.

Bromden is sliding along the hallway wall when he is suddenly cut off by a mop which THUDS against one side of his neck. A second mop yokes him on the other side. Bromden freezes. Terrified.

                    MILLER
         Where you goin', Chief?

                    WARREN
         You goin' t'see the Big White Fathuh?

> WASHINGTON
> He goin' t'see the Big White Muthuh ...

They cackle, legs jiving, as the ammonia stings Bromden's eyes and burns his nose. He tries to twist his head, but Washington jams the mop harder. Bromden freezes, panic spreading across his face.

> WASHINGTON (CONT'D)
> Haw, look at 'im, big 'nough to eat apples off my head an' he mine me like a baby ...

A KEY is HEARD hitting the lock in the main door. Washington very adroitly releases Bromden, hands him the mop, and turns, along with Warren and Miller, to their duties, as BIG NURSE enters the ward.

> THREE ATTENDANTS
> (simultaneously, as Big Nurse passes)
> Mornin', Miss Ratched ...

> BIG NURSE
> Good morning, boys.

She sweeps by and disappears into the nurses' station. The three attendants put their mops and rags aside and start towards the men's dorm, leaving Bromden pressed against the wall, mop in hand.

INT. NURSES' STATION

As Big Nurse enters to be greeted by Miss Pilbow, who wears an enormous cross between her breasts.

> MISS PILBOW
> Good morning, Miss Ratched. It's a beautiful day, isn't it?

                    BIG NURSE
          Mean old Monday, Miss Pilbow, mean old
          Monday...
              (she flips on the intercom)
          Good morning, boys. Rise and shine. Rise
          and shine.

INT. MEN'S DORM - DAY

As Washington, Warren and Miller roust the patients out of bed.

                    BIG NURSE (VO)
              (through loudspeaker)
          Time to get up! Come on now, it's a
          beautiful day! Let's not straggle!
          Everybody up, up, up!

The Chronics are physically helped out of bed as the Acutes, who can handle themselves, cross out into the day room, rubbing the sleep out of their eyes. Big Nurse steps out of the nurses' station. Washington and Warren are hustling the patients toward the washroom.

Miller stays behind, stripping Blastic's bed and rolling up his mattress.

INT. DAY ROOM - DAY

As the Acutes straggle past Big Nurse.

                    BIG NURSE
          Good morning, Mister Sefelt ... Good
          morning, Mister Fredrickson. Good morning,
          Billy, I spoke to your mother last night
          and she sends her love ... Good morning,
          Mister Harding ... Good morning, Mister
          Cheswick. Mister Scanlon ...

Bromden comes drifting by, going in the opposite direction. Big Nurse takes his hand and reaches up and pats his face.

                    BIG NURSE (CONT'D)
          Oh, Mister Bromden ...
          (calling out) Mister Washington!

Washington comes running.

                    WASHINGTON
          Yes, Miss Ratched?

                    BIG NURSE
          Mister Washington, why don't we get a
          good head start on the day by shaving
          Mister Bromden and see if we can't avoid a
          disturbance.

                    WASHINGTON
          (taking Bromden by the hand)
          Yes, Miss Ratched ...

INT. WASHROOM - DAY

The patients are busy washing and shaving.

Warren is assisting a catatonic wash himself as Washington guides Bromden through a cage-like partition ... where an antique barber chair stands.

                    WASHINGTON
          (calling as he goes)
          Warren!

He sits Bromden down and straps his hands and legs in, then plugs the electric shaver in and turns it on and brings the BUZZING instrument towards Bromden's face. Bromden turns away.

                    WASHINGTON (CONT'D)
          (shouting out)
          Get your black ass in here!

Warren props the vegetable up against the sink.

                    WARREN
          Tha's it ... be right back!

Warren leaves; the old man starts sliding.

                              QUICK CUT TO:

BROMDEN

As Warren enters and takes a firm grip on
Bromden's head and Washington goes to work on
Bromden's face. CAMERA PUSHES INTO EXTREME CLOSE-
UP of Bromden's fearfully distorted face as the
BUZZING SOUND of the electric razor INTENSIFIES
until it is INSUPPORTABLE.

                              QUICK CUT TO:

INT. DAY ROOM - DAY

No sound as we SEE Big Nurse watch the last few
patients file past the side door to the nurses'
station where Miss Pilbow hands out little cups
with pills. Washington stands by, checking to
see each man takes his pills before filling
their cups with orange juice.

The last patient takes his pills and returns to
his place in the day room. Miss Pilbow closes
the window.

Satisfied that all is well, Big Nurse turns
on an old 45 record player with a stack of
records, then she settles down to her work as
a SOFT, NOSTALGIC NUMBER from the 40s is HEARD
OVER LOUDSPEAKER.

CAMERA BEGINS SLOW PAN of the day room.

The patients, under the influence of drugs, have
settled down for the day. HARDING is playing
cards with MARTINI, CHESWICK and BILLY. SEFELT

and FREDRICKSON are putting a jigsaw puzzle together in brotherly love. SORENSEN is off by himself, rubbing his hands clean. TABER, pencil in hand, sits pondering over a blank piece of paper. SCANLON paces back and forth. On the Chronics' side of the room, RUCKLY is turning a grimy photograph over in his hands. BANCINI sits wagging his head, mumbling over and over, "Tired, awful tired ..." ELLIS stands against the wall, arms outstretched, hands nailed to the wall by imaginary nails. Bromden is pushing a mop around. Washington, Warren and Miller are in the men's dorm making up the Chronics' beds when OFF-SCREEN (OS) the TELEPHONE RINGS.

CUT TO:

INT. NURSES' STATION - DAY

As Miss Pilbow picks up the phone.

      MISS PILBOW
 Eighty-two, Miss Pilbow speaking ...
 Yes ...
 (she makes a note and hangs it)
 New admission, Miss Ratched ...

Miss Pilbow goes to the mirror, quickly preens herself, then turns and flips the intercom on.

      MISS PILBOW (CONT'D)
 (over loudspeaker)
 Mister Washington! Mister Warren!

She exits.

CUT TO:

INT. DAY ROOM

As Miss Pilbow exits nurses' station and heads down the hallway, Washington and Warren on her heels, Miller looking wistfully after them.

CUT TO: INT. MAIN ENTRANCE - STATE HOSPITAL - DAY

Staff personnel are SEEN moving in and out of the main entrance where a state penitentiary car is parked. A DEPUTY SHERIFF leans on the fender smoking a cigarette as SECOND DEPUTY SHERIFF comes out of the building and motions down to First Deputy, who crushes his cigarette out, then opens the rear door to the car.

                    DEPUTY SHERIFF
  (to an unseen occupant)
  Okay, let's go.

A long beat, then McMurphy slowly emerges from the car. He's wearing handcuffs and dressed in faded jeans, flannel work shirt, leather jacket, black motorcycle cap, and heavy black boots. He's been scrubbed clean and has a Band-Aid on his cheek. McMurphy does a couple of knee bends to get the kinks out of his legs as Deputy reaches in the car and takes out a small gym bag containing McMurphy's belongings.

                    DEPUTY SHERIFF (CONT'D)
  Let's move it ...

McMurphy goes up the stairs, followed by the Deputy, and crosses into the building.

INT. MAIN BUILDING - DAY

As McMurphy enters the building followed by the Deputies, where Nurse Pilbow, McMurphy's folder in hand, and Washington and Warren stand waiting - all in a pleasant, receptive mood. First Deputy hands McMurphy's gym bag to Washington, who hands it to Warren.

                    SECOND DEPUTY
  Okay, this is it!

McMurphy turns and holds out his hands. As cuffs are removed, McMurphy impulsively takes hold of the Deputy's head and plants a kiss on his forehead.

> SECOND DEPUTY (CONT'D)
> (squirming out of McMurphy's grasp)
> Jesus, you're crazy, McMurphy.

> McMURPHY
> Yeah, ain't that the truth.

> DEPUTY SHERIFF
> (to Miss Pilbow)
> He's all yours, Miss.

> MISS PILBOW
> Thank you, Officer ...

The two Deputies start down the stairs.

> McMURPHY
> So long, fellas...

The two Deputies merely shrug their shoulders at McMurphy, who takes a deep breath of fresh air.

> McMURPHY (CONT'D)
> Yes, sir, it's a mighty nice fall day ...

> MISS PILBOW
> This way, Mister McMurphy.

> McMURPHY
> Yes, ma'am ...

McMurphy follows Nurse Pilbow into the hallway as the door closes behind them.

CUT TO:

INT. HALLWAY - DAY

Other STAFF MEMBERS who are administrative personnel are SEEN as McMurphy walks alongside Nurse Pilbow, who is noticeably nervous by his close proximity. Washington and Warren casually bringing up the rear.

> McMURPHY
> (as he peels the Band-Aid off, revealing a scar)
> I tell ya, these goons showered me at the courthouse this morning, last night at the jail, and I swear they'd have swabbed my ears out on the way over if they could've found the facilities ...

A young Japanese nurse, named ITSU, passes by.

> McMURPHY (CONT'D)
> (to Nurse Itsu)
> Hey, how ya doin', cutie?

> NURSE ITSU
> Okay. How you doing?

> McMURPHY
> Just great!
> (calling after her)
> See ya around!

Nurse Itsu laughs and disappears around the corner.

> McMURPHY (CONT'D)
> (to Nurse Pilbow)
> Yes, sir, I sure am gonna enjoy my stay here.

> MISS PILBOW
> I'm sure you will.

> McMURPHY
> (to Nurse Pilbow)
> Ya know, I ain't never been in an institution of psychology before.

                    MISS PILBOW
          Oh ...

They arrive at the ward door. Nurse Pilbow
unlocks the door and opens it as ...

                    McMURPHY
          Yeah, I'm here on a ninety-day observation
          period. Short-timer, like they say ...

Soft nostalgic MUSIC is HEARD OVER.

                    MISS PILBOW
          Of course.
                (indicating door)
          Mister McMurphy.

                    McMURPHY
          After you, ma'am.

                    MISS PILBOW
          Thank you.

Nurse Pilbow enters the ward and McMurphy
watches her cross the visitors' area to a heavy-
gauge steel screen wall, with security gate,
which she opens.

                    McMURPHY
                (to Washington and Warren as they step into
                ward)
          Man, there sure is an awful lot of poontang
          around here.

                    SPIVEY
                (calling)
          Hold it!

McMurphy turns to see DOCTOR SPIVEY approaching.

                    SPIVEY (CONT'D)
          Good morning, boys.

                    WASHINGTON AND WARREN
          (simultaneously as Spivey passes into the
          ward)
          Mornin', Doctor Spivey.

                    SPIVEY
          Great day for fishing.

                    WASHINGTON AND WARREN
          (simultaneously)
          Yes, sir!

The door closes. CAMERA HOLDS on sign that READS:

SMILE AT THE NEXT FACE YOU SEE. IT MAY SAVE HIS LIFE.

                    McMURPHY (OS)
          Yeah, I was just thinking the same thing, Doc ...

                                        CUT TO:

INT. WARD - DAY

As McMurphy, Spivey, Washington and Warren cross the visitors' area towards Nurse Pilbow, who stands holding the security gate open. At the far end of the hallway, which opens into the day room, patients can be seen.

                    SPIVEY
          (to McMurphy)
          Oh, what's that?

                    McMURPHY
          Why, I'll betcha there must be a million
          albacore and tuna running off the coast
          right this minute.

                    SPIVEY
          Oh, do you do much fishing?

As they pass through the security gate:

                    McMURPHY
    Fish! Hell, Doc, I'd like to have a nickel
    for every fish I landed between Point
    Conception and the Alaska coast ...

Washington and Warren continue down the hallway,
passing SEFELT, who shyly approaches and waits
at a respectful distance.

                    SPIVEY
        (to McMurphy)
    Is that so?

                    McMURPHY
    Yup! Worked right outta Depoe Bay for just
    about every season since I was able to haul
    my own weight.

                    SPIVEY
    My, my ... Ah, who are you?

                    McMURPHY
    McMurphy, Doc. RP McMurphy.

They shake hands.

                    NURSE PILBOW
    Mister McMurphy is a new admission.

                    SPIVEY
    Ah, yes. Well, we must talk soon, Mister
    McMurphy.

                    McMURPHY
    You bet, Doc.

                    SPIVEY
    Good morning, Jim. How are you feeling?

                    SEFELT
        (approaching and pointing to his mouth)
    Doc, my gungs hurt me.

Spivey starts checking out Sefelt's mouth.

> NURSE PILBOW
> This way, Mister McMurphy.

As McMurphy follows Nurse Pilbow down the hall, Spivey's voice trails after him.

> SPIVEY (OS)
> Have you been taking your Dilantin, Jim?

> SEFELT (OS)
> Uh-huh ...

> SPIVEY (OS)
> Well, we'll send you over to the dentist and see what he can do. Okay?

> SEFELT (OS)
> Okay, Doc!

McMurphy and Nurse Pilbow reach the day room.

> MISS PILBOW
> Make yourself at home, Mister McMurphy ...

> McMURPHY
> Thank you, ma'am.

Nurse Pilbow enters the nurses' station, closing the door behind her. Next to the door is a bulletin board which, among other bits of information, READS:

TODAY IS MONDAY SEPTEMBER 30, 1963. THE NEXT MEAL IS LUNCH. THE NEXT HOLIDAY IS HALLOWEEN.

Another notice READS:

SIGN UP NOW! BASKETBALL TOURNAMENT STAFF VS PATIENTS.

Washington, Warren, Miller

There are no other names listed. Sefelt passes by.

> McMURPHY (CONT'D)
> Hi.

> SEFELT
> Hi.

Sefelt crosses into the day room where he joins Fredrickson, who is putting a jigsaw puzzle together.

INT. DAY ROOM - DAY

As McMurphy drifts into the room and looks around. The room is as it was. The MUSIC ENDS. There is a CLICK. McMurphy's attention is drawn to the nurses' station.

McMURPHY'S POV OF NURSES' STATION

Where Miss Pilbow is SEEN through a large plate glass window, busy typing a nameplate for McMurphy.

Big Nurse, her back to McMurphy, is turning over a stack of records. She presses the phonograph button. A record falls on the turntable and MUSIC BEGINS as she turns and sees McMurphy.

ANOTHER ANGLE

McMurphy smiles and tips his hat to Big Nurse. Big Nurse smiles back and takes her seat.

McMurphy turns and drifts into the day room. Big Nurse looks up and studies him.

Extract ends

---

http://sfy.ru/sfy.html?script=one_flew

As you can see from the above extract, the screenwriter has written many more pieces of dialogue than the director decided to use. Also a number of less important characters have been left out.

Much of the 14 or so pages of script above were slashed in production to create a tight six minutes of film without much dialogue as such. Yet the director's take of the original script still conveys the same information which the scriptwriter spelled out more wordily. The main characters are introduced – Nurse Ratched, McMurphy and Bromden, the Native American, whose presence was felt visually rather than spelled out verbally in the director's visualisation. Also the back story, which the scriptwriter described in the opening prison scene, was made accessible to the audience through the presence of the guards, the cuffs and McMurphy's behaviour.

More information about McMurphy's background and those of the patients is provided as the film progresses. The director stays closer to the written script later on, but I wanted to show you the discrepancy between written film and the visualised product at this point in the hope that you will write a script that is **visualised** well from the start. There is nothing wrong with the script of *One Flew Over the Cuckoo's Nest* as it is written. I think we have to admit, though, that the dramatic impact of the opening six minutes of the actual film is much stronger because of the exclusion of bitty scenes and much of the dialogue.

This is what you should aim for: a script that creates visual images that can translate immediately to film and that uses dialogue sparingly and only when it is essential. I will examine two more films to highlight the visual aspect of film writing.

Fur: An Imaginary Portrait of Diane Arbus

One film I find visually intriguing is *Fur: An Imaginary Portrait of Diane Arbus* (2006), written by Erin Cressida Wilson from the book by Patricia Bosworth. It is directed by Steven Shainberg. If you can find a copy of this film, watch the opening minutes especially and see how the whole landscape of the film is set up within a few shots. There isn't a copy of the script online but do try to watch it if you can. Its opening moments are perfect to show how much information can be conveyed visually in a few well-chosen scenes. I must warn you that this film isn't everyone's cup of tea, but I thought it was very creative visually.

Lost in Translation

Sofia Coppola's film *Lost in Translation* (2003) is written very visually. It's obvious it was written by a director-writer rather than a writer-writer, if you know what I mean. Look at the extract from the script below. Read it with close attention to how Coppola has written each scene to tell a visual story. Notice how the dialogue, when there is any, is almost inconsequential.

Extract begins

```
                                          FADE IN:

EXT. NARITA AIRPORT - NIGHT

We hear the sound of a plane landing over black.

                                          CUT TO:

INT. CHARLOTTE'S ROOM - NIGHT

The back of a GIRL in pink underwear, she leans
at a big window, looking out over Tokyo.

                                          CUT TO:

Melodramatic music swells over the Girl's butt
in pink sheer underwear as she lies on the bed.

TITLE CARDS OVER IMAGE.

                  LOST IN TRANSLATION

INT. CAR - NIGHT

POV from a car window - the colours and lights
of Tokyo neon at night blur by.

                                          CUT TO:
```

In the backseat of a Presidential limousine, BOB (late forties), tired and depressed, leans against a little doily, staring out the window.

POV from car window - We see buildings covered in bright signs, a billboard of Brad Pitt selling jeans, another of Bob in black & white, looking distinguished with a bottle of whiskey in a Suntory ad ... more signs, a huge TV with perky Japanese pop stars singing.

CUT TO:

EXT. PARK HYATT - NIGHT

Bob's black Presidential (looks like a 60s diplomat's car) pulls up at the entrance of the Park Hyatt, a modern sky rise.

The automatic doors open on the car, as Bob gets out.

Eager BELLHOPS with white gloves approach at the sight of the car, welcoming Bob and helping him with his bags.

CUT TO:

INT. PARK HYATT - NIGHT

Bob stands in the back of a crowded elevator surrounded by Japanese businessmen below his shoulders.

The elevator stops at the 50th floor and the doors open onto the massive, streamline lobby of the Park Hyatt.

Bob follows the JAPANESE BUSINESSMEN out into the marble and glass lobby that frames the view of Tokyo.

The CONCIERGE and several eager HOTEL MANAGERS greet Bob. He just wants to sleep, but more STAFF continue to greet him, ask him about his flight. They lead him to reception.

INT. HOTEL RECEPTION - NIGHT

At the reception area four JAPANESE BUSINESSMEN and two WOMEN quickly sit up from their seats on sight of Bob, and extend handshakes and gifts. They bow and introduce themselves from the commercial company, extend name cards and welcome him enthusiastically.

More staff welcomes him and offer their service during his stay.

One of them presents a fax that has come for him.

                                              INSERT:

"TO: BOB HARRIS FROM: LYDIA HARRIS

YOU FORGOT ADAM'S BIRTHDAY. I'M SURE HE'LL UNDERSTAND. HAVE A GOOD TRIP, L"

He doesn't know what to do with it, and stuffs it in his pocket.

The commercial people tell him when they'll be picking him up, and ask if he needs anything else.

Some JAPANESE ROCK STARS with shag haircuts and skinny leather pants pass by. Each commercial person has to shake Bob's hand before leaving.

                                              CUT TO:

INT. BOB'S HOTEL ROOM - NIGHT

Bob sits on the end of the bed in a too small hotel kimono.

INT. PARK HYATT BAR - NIGHT

Bob sits at the bar. A few minutes pass as he sits in silence looking around, drinking a scotch. Chet Baker sings The Thrill is Gone over the stereo.

We see Bob's POV of tables of people talking. JAPANESE WOMEN SMOKING, AMERICAN BUSINESSMEN tying one on, talking about software sales. A WAITER carefully setting down a coaster, and pouring a beer very, very slowly. It's all very foreign.

                                        CUT TO:

INT. BOB'S HOTEL ROOM - MORNING

The automatic hotel curtains open, pouring light into the room.

                                        CUT TO:

INT. HOTEL BATHROOM - DAY

Bob gets in the shower overlooking the view of Tokyo. The shower head is at his elbows. He raises it as high as it goes, and leans down to have a shower. This hotel was not designed with him in mind.

                                        CUT TO:

INT. STUDIO - DAY

Whiskey commercial shoot.

The set is full of activity as the JAPANESE CREW work.

Bob, in a shawl collared tuxedo sits at a European style bar set with a cut crystal glass of whiskey.

A JAPANESE GIRL quickly powders his face as they adjust lights and the DIRECTOR and crew speak in hurried Japanese.

The Director (with blue contact lenses) says a few long sentences in Japanese.

TRANSLATOR, a middle-aged woman in a coordinated outfit, translates but it is only a short sentence now.

                   TRANSLATOR
  He wants you to turn, look in camera and say the lines.

Bob wonders what she's leaving out, or if that's the way it works from Japanese to English.

                   BOB
  That's all he said?

                   TRANSLATOR
  Yes, turn to camera.

Bob thinks let's just get it over with.

                   BOB
  Turn left or right?

The Translator blots her face with a tissue, and asks the director in a Japanese sentence five times as long. The Director answers her in a long, excited phrase.

                   TRANSLATOR
  Right side. And with intensity.

                   BOB
  Is that everything? It seemed like he was saying a lot more.

The excited Director says more in Japanese. Translator nods in understanding. Bob doesn't really know what's going on.

                TRANSLATOR
  Like an old friend, and into the camera.

                DIRECTOR
  (to Bob)
  Suntory Time!

They get ready, and roll camera:

Bob turns and looks suavely to the camera:

                BOB
  For relaxing times, make it Suntory Time.

The Director yells something about ten sentences long. The translator nods.

                TRANSLATOR
  Could you do it slower, and with more intensity?

                BOB
  Okay.

The Translator answers for him in four sentences.

ON THE MONITOR - we see the next take: the moody lighting shines on Bob, the camera gets closer as he stares into camera and gives them the line.

                BOB
  For relaxing times, make it Suntory Time.

                              CUT TO:

EXT. TOKYO - NIGHT

Shinjuku High rises sparkle.

INT. PARK HYATT BAR - NIGHT

Tall glass walls show the neon and high-rises of the city.

A sad and romantic Bill Evans song plays. Bob sits alone with a scotch at the bar.

Some drunk AMERICAN BUSINESSMEN, with their ties thrown over their shoulders recognise him.

                  BUSINESS GUY
  Hey - you're Bob Harris - you're awesome, man.

                ANOTHER BUSINESS GUY
  Yeah, I love Sunset Odds!

                      BOB
  Oh, Ok, thanks.

                  BUSINESS GUY
  Man, that car-chase -

Bob nods.

INT. BOB'S HOTEL ROOM - NIGHT

Bob comes back to his room. The maids have left everything perfect, his beige bed is turned down, and the TV has been left on to a channel playing a montage of flower close-ups in nature while sad violin music plays. It's supposed to be relaxing, but it's just sad.

                                    CUT TO:

Bob lies in bed. He flips through TV channels from the remote control. He passes a Japanese game show, to an 80s Cannonball Run-type movie with him in it dubbed into Japanese. He turns it off as he hears a knock at the door.

He goes to the door, and opens it part way.

                    WOMAN (OC)
          (Raspy Japanese voice)
          Mr Harris?

                    BOB
          Yes?

                    WOMAN
          Mr Kazuzo sent me.

                    BOB
          Oh?

                    WOMAN
          Can I enter?

He pauses, then opens the door.

A WOMAN in her forties in a short tight leather mini skirt and stockings comes in. She is wearing 60s style make-up.

Bob sits on the bed not sure what to do as he watches her.

Bob's POV - We see her back to us as she puts a CD on the stereo - it begins to play: Serge Gainsberg and Brigitte Bardot sing Bonnie & Clyde. The woman turns slyly around and shimmies over to Bob.

                    WOMAN
          (as she tries to undress him)
          Mr Harris?

                    BOB
          Yes?

                    WOMAN
          Do you like massage?

                    BOB
          I don't think so.

                        WOMAN
        Mr Kazuzo send Premium Fantasy.

She pushes him back onto the bed. He hesitates,
but then goes along with it passively.

                        WOMAN
        My stockings.

                        BOB
        Yes?

                        WOMAN
        Take them.

He fumbles with her stockings, trying to do as
she says.

                        WOMAN
        No - Lip them ... Don't touch me!

He takes his hands back confused.

                        WOMAN
        Lip my stockings!

He backs away, as he tries to understand her.

                        WOMAN
        Lip them!

She throws her leg up to him on the bed.

                        BOB
        Huh?

She pantomimes ripping them. He finally
understands.

                        BOB
        Oh, you want me to rip them?

He pulls at her stockings trying to rip them, but they just snap.

She pretends to struggle.

              WOMAN
  Please let me go!

He pulls his hands away. She grabs them and puts them back on her, and keeps struggling dramatically. They wrestle around awkwardly, her pretending to try to get away, but not letting him go. She rips her stockings and falls off the bed in fake-defence.

              WOMAN
  Let me go!

She pulls a confused Bob down on top of her. He doesn't know what she wants.

She rips another stocking and pins him on the ground. He tries to crawl away, she grabs his leg and trips him. He grabs a nearby table leg as he falls, the lamp crashes to the floor, the room goes black.

              BOB
  I think you should leave.

                            CUT TO:

INT. HOTEL RESTAURANT - DAY

In the harsh sunlight of the big windows Bob eats breakfast alone. Next to him is a table of TEXANS in cowboy hats. At another table a JAPANESE COUPLE in sunglasses chain smoke and drink coffee.

                            CUT TO:

INT. HOTEL ELEVATOR - DAY

Bob gets into the elevator. He is stopped momentarily by the Concierge who asks him if everything is fine for his stay.

In the elevator Bob's surrounded by JAPANESE BUSINESSPEOPLE and a FAMILY dressed for a wedding.

Across, at the other side of the elevator he sees CHARLOTTE, a pretty Ivy-League girl in her mid-twenties, and the only other Westerner in the elevator. Her honey-coloured hair stands out in the crowd.

She's looking at him like you do when someone new comes in the elevator, but the Japanese look straight ahead at the elevator doors.

Charlotte and Bob look at each other across the Japanese heads. She smiles, from one foreigner to another. The door opens and she gets out with the crowd. Bob watches her leave.

                    MISS KAWASAKI
  Mr Harris.

He is approached by a group of eight excited people from the commercial company there waiting to take him.

                    PRESS AGENT
  (as they are on their way)
  We just got a request from Tanabe Mori –
  he is the Johnny Carson of Japan! It is a
  big honour to be invited to his show.

Bob feigns enthusiasm briefly.

                    MISS KAWASAKI
  Can you stay until Friday?

                    BOB
          I'll have to see about that.

                                              CUT TO:

INT. PHOTO STUDIO - DAY

Bob's back is to us as a MAKE-UP ARTIST
is putting some final touches on him. The
PHOTOGRAPHER is giving her enthusiastic direction
in Japanese. Bob talks on his cell phone, not
paying attention to the make-up artist.

                    BOB
          Can you get me on a flight Thursday night?

                    ELAINE (OS)
          We're looking into it, Bob, but they really
          want you to stay to do that talk show
          Friday, apparently it's a really big deal,
          he's the Johnny Carson of Japan.

                    BOB
          Yeah, they told me.

                    ELAINE (OS)
          These people are paying you a lot, do you
          think you could consider it?

                    BOB
          Just get me out of here as soon as you can.

                    ELAINE (OS)
          Ok, you're scheduled to leave Saturday, but
          we'll hold a seat Thursday in case, but first
          class is full, you're waitlisted for an upgrade
          ... there might be a seat on Lufthansa ...

                    BOB
          Oh, great. I'll talk to you later, bye.

He hangs up. The make-up artist dusts him with
powder.

The commercial people are crowding around. Bob's chair is swivelled around and we see him in his tuxedo, wearing too much make-up and some weird-looking eyeliner.

In front of a grey backdrop, moody lighting is being adjusted and Bob is handed a bottle of Suntory.

A small documentary crew moves in on Bob with a video camera. The camera man is tilting the camera at his face in arty Dutch camera moves.

The agency people crowd around. The photographer is excited and urges Bob to do dumb poses, he won't do.

                    PHOTOGRAPHER
          Can you put hands close to face?

The photographer demonstrates a dramatic pose with his hands at his face.

                    BOB
          Urn, I don't think so. How bout I just hold the bottle.

The photographer starts shooting. Bob obviously hates the whole thing, what you do for money.

                                        CUT TO:

INT. PARK HYATT BAR - NIGHT

Bob, still in his tuxedo and make-up from the shoot, sits alone having a drink.

A JAZZ BAND FROM SAUSALITO performs.

The SINGER is a middle-aged woman with red wavy hair, dressed in red, and takes her singing very seriously. She sings a slow version of "Parsley, Sage, Rosemary and Thyme".

CU - a golden beer is poured very slowly.

Bob drinks his scotch, hoping it will all go away.

Across the bar, Charlotte sits with JOHN, her husband (he is in his late twenties and sloppy in a fashionable way), and some FRIENDS - super stylish, weird Japanese fashion people (all smoking). One of them, CHARLIE, in a shiny suit, keeps taking pictures, and showing them magazine layouts.

                  JAZZ SINGER
  Thank you. We're glad to be here, we're Sausalito.

Charlotte laughs and looks down, the Japanese audience clap very seriously ... she and Bob catch eyes - about Sausalito and how weird it is there.

                                      CUT TO:

INT. ELEVATOR - LATER

The mirrored elevator doors close and Bob sees himself close up in the elevator's mirrored walls - noticing the heavy makeup and weird eyeliner from the shoot which he had forgotten about. He looks at himself.

                                      CUT TO:

INT. CHARLOTTE'S HOTEL ROOM - NIGHT

Charlotte lays close to her young husband, John. She looks to see if he's awake, but he's sleeping soundly. She leans her chin on his shoulder.

                  CHARLOTTE
  Are you awake?

He doesn't answer.

                         CHARLOTTE
            John?

He grumbles something, opens one sleepy eye to
look at her, and grabs her under the covers. He
kisses her.

                         JOHN
            Go to sleep.

He holds her close, but she can't sleep.

                                        CUT TO:

Charlotte sits on a ledge looking out at the big
buildings.

The sun is starting to come up. Below she
watches cars going places.

                                        CUT TO:

INT. BOB'S HOTEL ROOM - NIGHT

Bob lies in bed awake. The clock says 4:20.

The in-room fax machine is making noise as a
fax rolls in. Bob looks at the fax machine but
doesn't get out of bed.

The fax curls and falls to the floor.

CLOSE ON FAX -

"BOB - YOU DIDN'T TELL ME WHICH SHELVES YOU WANT
IN YOUR STUDY. PLEASE PICK ONE OUT AND LET ME
KNOW. I'M HAVING LOTS OF QUALITY TIME WITH THE
CONSTRUCTION CREW. HOPE YOU'RE HAVING FUN THERE.
LOVE, L"

Three pages of shelf diagrams follow.

                                        CUT TO:

INT. HOTEL GYM - NIGHT

The gym is empty except for an old man vacuuming. Bob passes piles of little towels and bottles of water. He takes a water for his workout.

He approaches an exercise machine and puts the water in the drink holder of the machine. He looks at the lit-up instruction panel - it is all in Japanese. He pushes a button, and the machine starts beeping, then a soothing woman's voice recites instructions in Japanese.

He gets on it, and sinks. He tries to make the arms and foot pedals coordinate. He pushes a button and it starts moving too fast. In an upward rotation he tries to reach the control panel, but is not fast enough.

The soothing woman's voice continues instruction. She occasionally includes an English word - gently, gently ... vigorous. He tries to keep up with it, and tries again to push the right button to slow it down, but the machine steps start going swiftly backwards instead.

CUT TO:

INT. PARK HYATT LOBBY (GROUND FLOOR) - DAY

The agency group waits for Bob. They stand up as he approaches from the elevator, trying to mask a slight limp.

                    BOB
  (everything's fine)
Good morning.

Miss Kawasaki notices his limp with concern as they leave the hotel.

CUT TO:

```
EXT. SHIBUYA STATION - DAY

Charlotte gets out at Shibuya station, a crowded
neighbourhood filled with neon, ads, and people.

She looks up at the huge intersection as tons of
JAPANESE PEOPLE wait to cross the street, no one
steps forward until the crosswalk light changes,
and all of them cross.

A TV screen covering a building plays
commercials.

She roams around the narrow streets, crowded with
stylish JAPANESE KIDS, tan SCHOOLGIRLS pass her.

                                              CUT TO:

Charlotte wanders down a crowded street, looking
around. On a small side street, she stops at
a little park. She watches a JAPANESE MAN AND
WOMAN together:

CHARLOTTE'S POV -

CU The man reaches his hand to the back of the
woman's neck, and leans in close. The woman
smiles at him, in love.
```

Extract ends

---

http://www.dailyscript.com/scripts/lost-in-translation-script.html

I included so much of this script because it is a perfect example of visual storytelling. The reason Sofia Coppola won the Best Script Oscar for this film is evident. Her humorous take on the culture clash of Westerners in an Eastern setting comes through so well in the scenes she describes. If you haven't seen this film, it is well worth watching. It's a great example of telling a story through the medium of film.

Think of other films you have seen and decide how effectively they were written – visually well executed or not.

But what about *Notting Hill*?

It is a fact that British films tend to have much more dialogue than American films. It is also a fact that I tend to prefer British films. Funnily enough, I also love writing dialogue.

There are many verbose and successful films on our screens. Some have been adapted for screen from stage plays, for example. *Proof* is one such film which was made in 2005. The film script was written by Rebecca Miller, based on David Auburn's Pulitzer Prize-winning play, and it achieved some success at the box office. The fact that it had Anthony Hopkins and Gwyneth Paltrow in the lead roles may have helped its success too.

Frost and Nixon (2006) is another example of an intellectual debate portrayed on screen. Written by Peter Morgan for both the stage and screen, it is a compelling film, which has more than its fair share of words. Unusually for a film made in America, it is dialogue-driven rather than action-driven. Perhaps it is a result of the tarnished reputation of Richard Nixon that the film was so popular. Or maybe it was the skill of the exceptional writer, Peter Morgan, who also wrote *The Queen* (2006) and *The Last King of Scotland* (2006). It seems he has mastered the art of the modern biopic.

There are other British film writers who are exceptionally good at the dialogue-driven screenplay. One of these is my favourite romantic comedy writer, Richard Curtis. It's reassuring to see that extracts from his scripts look as wordy as some of mine.

Here is a brief example from an oldie but a goodie, *Notting Hill* (1999):

Extract begins

```
EXT. PORTOBELLO ROAD - DAY

                    WILLIAM (VO)
     So this is where I spend my days and years
     - in this small village in the middle of a
     city - in a house with a blue door that my
     wife and I bought together ... before she
     left me for a man who looked like Harrison
     Ford, only even handsomer ...
```

We arrive outside his blue-doored house just off Portobello.

> WILLIAM (VO)
> ... and where I now lead a strange half-life with a lodger called ...

INT. WILLIAM'S HOUSE – DAY

> WILLIAM
> Spike!

The house has far too many things in it. Definitely two-bachelors' flat.

Spike appears. An unusual-looking fellow. He has unusual hair, unusual facial hair and an unusual Welsh accent: very white, as though his flesh has never seen the sun. He wears only shorts.

> SPIKE
> Even he. Hey, you couldn't help me with an incredibly important decision, could you?

> WILLIAM
> This is important in comparison to, let's say, whether they should cancel third world debt?

> SPIKE
> That's right – I'm at last going out on a date with the great Janine and I just want to be sure I've picked the right t-shirt.

> WILLIAM
> What are the choices?

> SPIKE
> Well ... wait for it ...
> (He pulls on a T-shirt)
> First there's this one ...

The T-shirt is white with a horrible looking plastic alien coming out of it, jaws open, blood everywhere. It says, "I Love Blood".

                WILLIAM
Yes – might make it hard to strike a really romantic note.

                SPIKE
Point taken.

He heads back up the stairs ... talks as he changes ...

                SPIKE
I suspect you'll prefer the next one.

And he re-enters in a white T-shirt, with a large arrow, pointing down to his flies, saying, "Get It Here".

                SPIKE
Cool, huh?

                WILLIAM
Yes – she might think you don't have true love on your mind.

                SPIKE
Wouldn't want that ...
(and back up he goes)
Okay – just one more.

He comes down wearing it. Lots of hearts, saying, "You're the most beautiful woman in the world."

                WILLIAM
Well, yes, that's perfect. Well done.

                SPIKE
Thanks. Great. Wish me luck.

> WILLIAM
> Good luck.

Spike turns and walks upstairs proudly. Revealing that on the back of the T-shirt, also printed in big letters, is written "Fancy a fuck?"

EXT. PORTOBELLO ROAD – DAY

> WILLIAM (VO)
> And so it was just another hopeless Wednesday, as I set off through the market to work, little suspecting that this was the day which would change my life forever. This is work, by the way, my little travel book shop ...

A small unpretentious store ... named "The Travel Book Co" ...

> WILLIAM (VO)
> ... which, well, sells travel books – and, to be frank with you, doesn't always sell many of those.

William enters.

INT. THE BOOKSHOP – DAY

It is a small shop, slightly chaotic, bookshelves everywhere, with little secret bits round corners with even more books.

Martin, William's sole employee, is waiting enthusiastically.

He is very keen, an uncrushable optimist. Perhaps without cause. A few seconds later, William stands gloomily behind the desk.

> WILLIAM
> Classic. Absolutely classic.
> Profit from major sales plus/minus £347.

                    MARTIN
          Shall I go get a cappuccino?
          Ease the pain.

                    WILLIAM
          Yes, better get me a half. All I can
          afford.

                    MARTIN
          I get your logic. Demi-capu coming up.

He salutes and bolts out the door – as he
does, a woman walks in. We only just glimpse
her.

                                         CUT TO

William working. He looks up casually. And sees
something. His reaction is hard to read. After a
pause ...

                    WILLIAM
          Can I help you?

It is Anna Scott, the biggest movie star in
the world – here – in his shop. The most
divine, subtle, beautiful woman on earth.
When she speaks she is very self-assured and
self-contained.

                    ANNA
          No, thanks. I'll just look around.

                    WILLIAM
          Fine.

She wanders over to a shelf as he watches her –
and picks out a quite smart coffee table book.

                    WILLIAM
          That book's really not good – just in case,
          you know, browsing turned to buying. You'd
          be wasting your money.

ANNA
Really?

WILLIAM
Yes. This one though is ... very good.

He picks up a book on the counter.

WILLIAM
I think the man who wrote it has actually been to Turkey, which helps. There's also a very amusing incident with a kebab.

ANNA
Thanks. I'll think about it.

William suddenly spies something odd on the small TV monitor beside him.

WILLIAM
If you could just give me a second.

Her eyes follow him as he moves toward the back of the shop and approaches a man in slightly ill-fitting clothes.

WILLIAM
Excuse me.

THIEF
Yes.

WILLIAM
Bad news.

THIEF
What?

WILLIAM
We've got a security camera in this bit of the shop.

                         THIEF
So?

                        WILLIAM
So, I saw you put that book down your
trousers.

                         THIEF
What book?

                        WILLIAM
The one down your trousers.

                         THIEF
I haven't got a book down my trousers.

                        WILLIAM
Right - well, then we have something of
an impasse. I tell you what, I'll call
the police - and, what can I say? - If
I'm wrong about the whole book-down-the-
trousers scenario, I really apologise.

                         THIEF
Okay - what if I did have a book down my
trousers?

                        WILLIAM
Well, ideally, when I went back to the
desk, you'd remove the *Cadogan Guide to
Bali* from your trousers, and either wipe
it and put it back, or buy it. See you in
a sec.

He returns to his desk. In the monitor we just
glimpse, as does William, the book coming out
of the trousers and put back on the shelves.
The thief drifts out towards the door. Anna,
who has observed all this, is looking at a
blue book on the counter.

> WILLIAM
> Sorry about that ...

> ANNA
> No, that's fine. I was going to steal one myself but now I've changed my mind. Signed by the author, I see.

> WILLIAM
> Yes, we couldn't stop him. If you can find an unsigned copy, it's worth an absolute fortune.

She smiles. Suddenly the thief is there.

> THIEF
> Excuse me.

> ANNA
> Yes.

> THIEF
> Can I have your autograph?

> ANNA
> What's your name?

> THIEF
> Rufus.

She signs his scruffy piece of paper. He tries to read it.

> THIEF
> What does it say?

> ANNA
> Well, that's the signature – and above, it says, "Dear Rufus – you belong in jail".

> THIEF
> Nice one. Would you like my phone number?

> ANNA
> Tempting but ... no, thank you.

Thief leaves.

ANNA
I think I will try this one.

She hands William a £20 note and the book he said was rubbish. He talks as he handles the transaction.

WILLIAM
Oh - right - on second thoughts maybe it wasn't that bad. Actually - it's a sort of masterpiece really. None of those childish kebab stories you get in so many travel books these days. And I'll throw in one of these for free.

He drops in one of the signed books.

WILLIAM
Very useful for lighting fires, wrapping fish, that sort of thing.

She looks at him with a slight smile.

ANNA
Thanks.

And leaves. She's out of his life forever. William is a little dazed. Seconds later Martin comes back in.

MARTIN
Cappuccino as ordered.

WILLIAM
Thanks. I don't think you'll believe who was just in here.

MARTIN
Who? Someone famous?

But William's innate natural English discretion takes over.

WILLIAM
No. No-one - no-one.

They set about drinking their coffees.

> MARTIN
> Would be exciting if someone famous did come into the shop though, wouldn't it? Do you know - this is pretty incredible actually - I once saw Ringo Starr. Or at least I think it was Ringo. It might have been that bloke from *Fiddler on the Roof*, Toppy.

> WILLIAM
> Topol.

> MARTIN
> That's right - Topol.

> WILLIAM
> But Ringo Starr doesn't look anything like Topol.

> MARTIN
> No, well ... he was quite a long way away.

> WILLIAM
> So it could have been neither of them?

> MARTIN
> I suppose so.

> WILLIAM
> Right. It's not a classic anecdote, is it?

> MARTIN
> Not classic, no.

Martin shakes his head. William drains his cappuccino.

> WILLIAM
> Right - want another one?

> MARTIN
> Yes. No, wait - let's go crazy - I'll have an orange juice.

Extract ends

http://www.awesomefilm.com/script/nothill.txt

Obviously, Richard Curtis' ability to write dialogue is brilliant. The broad rule with film dialogue, however, is that if an event or beat can be **shown** visually rather than **told**, write it visually. However, if you too can write dialogue that dances off the page, write dialogue where you think it fits.

And this brings me neatly to voiceover narration.

Voiceover Narration

Robert McKee regards the use of voiceover narration as the devil itself. To clarify, voiceover (VO) narration is the name given to the technique of allowing an **off-screen character** to provide a **commentary** to the **action** the audience sees on screen. To McKee, using a VO narrator is the equivalent of admitting defeat as a scriptwriter. He believes it is a cop-out to "tell" the audience what they should think while they watch action on screen. McKee believes VO narration is a sign that the writer has not mastered the art of film writing.

There is an excellent parody of Robert McKee in Charlie Kaufman's film *Adaptation* (2002). In one scene, the protagonist goes to a "McKee" workshop to try to find help for the script he's attempting to write. The film is about the adaptation of a novel Charlie Kaufman, the main character, has to write but isn't able to get to grips with. His character has been commentating on the action throughout in a VO narration from the first moments of the film. Going to the McKee workshop near the end of the second act is almost an admission of defeat for the protagonist. He has violently rejected the screenwriting guru, McKee, and his methods, in the face of his brother's strong recommendations.

The scene takes place when Kaufman (the character in the film – it's a very solipsistic film!) is in "McKee's" workshop. The VO narration continues while McKee writes a complicated set of screenwriting rules on an overhead projector.

We've already seen McKee ranting and strutting his stuff on the stage declaiming his theories as if he were Moses proclaiming the Ten Commandments. Now the packed auditorium is taking notes as Kaufman sweats profusely in his near-permanent state of existential angst.

Extract begins

INT. AUDITORIUM – LATER

                KAUFMAN (VO)
It is my weakness, my ultimate lack of conviction that brings me here. Easy answers. Rules to shortcut your way to success. And here I am, because my jaunt into the abyss has brought me nothing. Well, isn't that the risk one takes for attempting something new. I should leave here right now. I'll start over ...

           (he starts to rise)

        I need to face this project head on and ...

                McKEE
... and God help you if you use voiceover in your work my friends.

Kaufman looks up startled. McKee seems to be watching him.

              McKEE (CONT'D)
God help you! It's flaccid, sloppy writing. Any idiot can write voiceover narration to explain the thoughts of a character. You must present the internal conflicts of your character in action.

Kaufman looks at the people scribbling in notebooks. "Flaccid ..." writes the guy on one side of him. "Any idiot ..." writes the guy on the other side.

Extract ends

---

http://www.scribd.com/doc/2171461/Adaptation-Final-Script

I recommend reading the above version of the script, especially the "McKee" seminar from page 86 onwards. Apart from it being well written, it makes you realise that no-one has all the answers when it comes to scriptwriting.

Therefore, I believe the best way to treat VO narration is sparingly, unless you do it exceptionally well. If you think of films such as *The Shawshank Redemption* (1994), *Million Dollar Baby* (2004), *Notting Hill* and many other excellent films, the VO can add great value to a film. Just to prove my point it is worth including a wonderful example from the opening scenes of *Notting Hill*.

Extract begins

EXT. VARIOUS DAYS

(The song) "She" plays through the credits.

Exquisite footage of Anna Scott – the great movie star of our time – an ideal – the perfect star and woman – her life full of glamour and sophistication and mystery.

EXT. STREET - DAY

Mix through to William, 35, relaxed, pleasant, informal. We follow him as he walks down Portobello Road, carrying a loaf of bread. It is spring.

> WILLIAM (VO)
> Of course, I've seen her films and always thought she was, well, fabulous – but, you know, million miles from the world I live in. Which is here – Notting Hill – not a bad place to be ...

EXT. PORTOBELLO ROAD - DAY

It's a full fruit market day.

> WILLIAM (VO)
> There's the market on weekdays, selling every fruit and vegetable known to man ...

EXT. PORTOBELLO ROAD - DAY

A man in denims exits the tattoo studio.

> WILLIAM (VO)
> The tattoo parlour – with a guy outside who got drunk and now can't remember why he chose "I Love Ken" ...

EXT. PORTOBELLO ROAD - DAY

> WILLIAM (VO)
> The racial hairdressers where everyone comes out looking like the Cookie Monster, whether they like it or not ...

Sure enough, a girl exits with a huge threaded blue bouffant.

EXT. PORTOBELLO ROAD - SATURDAY

> WILLIAM (VO)
> Then suddenly it's the weekend, and from break of day, hundreds of stalls appear out of nowhere, filling Portobello Road right up to Notting Hill Gate ...

A frantic crowded Portobello market.

> WILLIAM (VO)
> ... and thousands of people buy millions of antiques, some genuine ...

The camera finally settles on a stall selling beautiful stained-glass windows of various sizes, some featuring biblical scenes and saints.

> WILLIAM (VO)
> ... and some not so genuine.

EXT. GOLBORNE ROAD - DAY

> WILLIAM (VO)
> And what's great is that lots of friends have ended up in this part of London – that's Tony, architect-turned-chef, who recently invested all the money he ever earned in a new restaurant ...

Shot of Tony proudly setting out a board outside his restaurant, the sign still being painted. He receives and approves a huge fresh salmon.

EXT. PORTOBELLO ROAD - DAY

> WILLIAM (VO)
> So this is where I spend my days and years – in this small village in the middle of a city in a house with a blue door that my wife and I bought together ... before she left me for a man who looked like Harrison Ford, only even handsomer ...

We arrive outside his blue-doored house just off Portobello.

> WILLIAM (VO)
> ... and where I now lead a strange half-life with a lodger called ...

INT. WILLIAM'S HOUSE - DAY

> WILLIAM
> Spike!

Extract ends

---

http://www.awesomefilm.com/script/nothill.txt

Perhaps there is nothing more to say than this: if voiceover narration seems like the best choice for your film, use it – but ensure you use it well.

4. Breaking it Down to Basics – Formatting Your Film

Now that you have written a beat sheet and the step outline, you have broken the back of the structure of your script. I hope you appreciate how important it is to complete a beat sheet before tackling writing a full script. I really believe in this process as it makes bite-sized chunks out of what could feel like an insurmountable task. If you break your story down step by step, starting with the beat sheet, which leads quite effortlessly to the step outline, you are so much more secure when it comes to writing the script itself.

I always tell my scriptwriting students that writing a good beat sheet is like using a pattern to cut and sew a dress. When I was an adolescent, I used to make dresses out of large pieces of beautiful silk. I'd cut and sew them as the mood took me, always without a pattern, and it's no wonder my mother often asked me to change before I visited her at her office!

You now have a very good pattern to use to create an excellent script.

I have a few friends who are playwrights and novelists who object to plotting a storyline so thoroughly before writing. They believe the muse should speak to them freely and lead them wherever their writing takes them. I answer their objections by saying that a writer may perhaps have the freedom to wander aimlessly wherever his/her fancy leads when writing prose and especially novels. It is also possible to write as many monologues or dialogues as you'd like when writing stage plays.

Film, however, does not allow for the luxury of rambling. No producer or director will have patience with a woolly script with self-indulgent dialogue. And if your plot meanders leisurely rather than moving swiftly along, no-one will commit millions of rands, dollars or pounds to make your film in the hope that it *may* turn out to be quite a good story in the end.

However, you, as a diligent student, have not meandered wildly but have been extremely disciplined in writing a tight beat sheet and step outline that follows the hero's journey to a greater or lesser extent. Now is the time to flesh out the bones of your step outline and allow your characters to take their first breaths.

Formatting the Script

Firstly, if you have a program such as Final Draft, your work is almost done for you. If not, all is not lost. You will be able to format your script using Microsoft Word by following the standard requirements for a script.

As you saw from the extracts above, there is a standard way of writing a script. The scripts such as *Cuckoo's Nest* are quite loosely formatted with a number of camera shots and angles included at times. However, unless you are an experienced filmwriter most directors will be annoyed if you are too prescriptive about the camera angles they should use. Your best bet is to leave that up to them. However, if you visualise the scenes that you want to write clearly and express your vision well, the director may be inspired by your vision. I work with one particular director who likes me to describe each scene in as much detail as possible so that he can start to visualise the way he will translate my vision into film. Be warned, however. Some directors do not like too much description.

Let's get started.

Title Page

Step one of writing your script will be to write a **working title** on the front page. If you have already decided on a definite **title** then use that. However, if you write Working Title in brackets beneath the title on the title page, the producer will know that you haven't quite decided on a definite one yet.

Underneath the title you will write **written by** with your name below it. If there are other writers working on the project, you must include their names too. If script editors have been used, their names should be listed below yours as such. Most producers also like to have the writer's contact details at the bottom of the title page too.

The title, your name and those of any other writers and script editors should be in the middle of the page with your contact details at the bottom.

Here is an example from a short film I wrote.

```
                        THE RED SHOES

                     Written by JANET VAN EEDEN

    Name: Janet van Eeden

    Address: Fever Tree House, # Taylor Road,
    Pietermaritzburg, 3201 Phone Number:
    ############
```

Font

It was a shock to me when I first found out how prescriptive directors and producers are about the font used in a screenplay. If it is not written in Courier or Courier Final Draft, in 12 point font, they will not read it.

If you use Final Draft, this is the font that is used automatically. If not, be sure to change your font's settings as soon as you start writing. All professional scripts are written in this font. I think it goes without saying that they are always written in black.

```
    This is an example of the font (Courier) in
    which your screenplay will be written. This
    is why, as you may have noticed, all extracts
    you've seen so far have been in this font.
    (Here the Courier font size is a little
    smaller than 12 point.)
```

The font used is so important and so much part of professional scriptwriting that one of the best scriptwriting websites in Britain is, in fact, called Twelvepoint.com.

You have no option but to write your script in Courier 12 point. If it isn't in this particular font, producers and directors will not even read the first page.

Scene Headings

The first page of your script starts with a scene heading. It is a good idea to number the pages if you are not using Final Draft or some other scriptwriting software that numbers the script automatically.

The **scene heading** gives the reader the information about whether the scene is taking place **inside** or **outside,** **where** the scene is taking place, and an approximation of the **time of day.**

The scene heading is always written in **CAPITAL LETTERS** and it hugs the left-hand margin. Here is an example from one of my short films *The Red Shoes.*

```
EXT. STREET PAVEMENT INNER CITY - SUNSET
```

The statement of whether the scene takes place in an Exterior or Interior setting is always abbreviated to EXT or INT. If the scene cuts between an exterior and interior at some points, you can write the scene heading in this way.

```
EXT/INT. SUBURBAN HOUSE - DAY
```

If a scene moves from the pavement, for example into a house, you would write the scene heading as follows:

```
EXT. STREET PAVEMENT/INT. SUBURBAN HOUSE
- SUNSET

(Continuous)
```

"Continuous" shows that the scene continues seamlessly from the exterior to the interior.

Numbers are not usually assigned to scene headings until the script is almost ready to be filmed. Then a **shooting script** will be finalised and the scene headings will be numbered. However, I have worked with a producer who wanted the scene headings numbered from the start. Always be prepared to adapt to the needs of each producer.

Action Lines

Action lines, which describe **what is happening on screen**, are lines of descriptive prose which explain to the reader what he or she can expect to see on screen. Action lines describe the action of the film.

The action lines follow one line beneath the scene headings and also hug the left-hand margin. Another example from *The Red Shoes*:

Extract begins

EXT. STREET PAVEMENT INNER CITY – SUNSET

The BRIGHT RED patent leather HEELS CLICK along the pavement, kick-starting the street LIGHTS into action. Each one flickers to life as the heels click past. The surrounding street is grey and dusty. The debris of the long, hot day drifts listlessly along the gutters: ragged PLASTIC BAGS; bits of gnawed chicken BONES; red and white KENTUCKY FRIED CHICKEN BOXES, crumpled in defeat; jagged edges of BROKEN BOTTLES; yesterday's NEWSPAPERS fluttering like white flags, signal surrender.

NOTHEMBA'S eyes scan the smog-smudged patch of orange SKY glimmering between the BUILDINGS at the end of the street.

Extract ends

You will see that I have written a number of words in CAPITALS in the body of the action lines. The capitals are there to draw the reader's attention to what should be visible on screen. In this way, I haven't reverted to telling the director that I would like to see a close-up of the red shoes, followed by close-ups of the debris on the city street, but I have drawn their attention to these details. It would be hard for a director to resist focusing on these objects, especially as they symbolise the dirty edges of society in which Nothemba lives.

The character's name, Nothemba, is also written in caps the first time her name is mentioned. This allows a producer to see the main characters quickly. It also allows an actor to scan a script looking for scenes which feature the character they will play. Some scripts keep using caps for the names of characters throughout the screenplay. I like to use caps for their first mention and then write them normally from then on. Once again, be informed by what a specific director or producer would prefer you to do.

You will also notice that I have been fairly descriptive about the surroundings in the above scene. It was important to me to convey the sense of hopelessness which the character feels through the urban decay. That is why the action lines are quite descriptive. Once again, notice that only objects that can be visualised and actions that can be executed are included in the action lines.

Dialogue

The action lines are followed by dialogue if you want your character to speak. Remember once again, to use dialogue only when it is essential and never for exposition or storytelling.

In the dialogue box, the character's name will be written in capital letters and centred on the page. Once again, a screenwriting program would format this for you. If you don't have such a program, simply centre your character's name and the dialogue that follows beneath the name.

Here is another example from *The Red Shoes* where I have included the action lines that precede the lines of dialogue as well as the action lines that follow them so that you can see how they fit together.

Extract begins

```
NOTHEMBA'S eyes scan the smog-smudged patch of
orange SKY glimmering between the BUILDINGS at
the end of the street. She whispers under her
breath.

                    NOTHEMBA
          (To herself, in Xhosa)
          Left, right, left, right. Keep walking and
          it will be alright.

She glances down at the SHOES as she walks. The
red leather is scuffed in places, and cracked at
the heels. Nothemba's 14-year-old feet slip in
```

```
them slightly as she walks, unused to the high
heels.
```

Extract ends

Parentheses

The **parentheses** (brackets) under Nothemba's name in the extract above gives us added information about the way Nothemba speaks her lines of dialogue. Parentheses can sometimes be used to convey some of the innermost thoughts of the characters but they should not be overused.

I had a tendency to put adverbs in brackets before each line of dialogue for quite a few years but producers, directors and actors tend to find this very annoying. I now restrict these to just a few adverbs per script. I think this must be the director in me dying to tell the actors how to say their lines.

Another point worth noting here is that I wrote this script imagining that any dialogue Nothemba and her family would have would be in Xhosa. Because I have only a rudimentary knowledge of Xhosa and most scriptwriters wouldn't be fluent in it either, I describe her dialogue as being in Xhosa in parentheses, and write the dialogue in English. Further down the line a translator would be called in to write the lines in Xhosa. English subtitles would be inserted in post-production. Telling the reader that these lines would be spoken in Xhosa, however, alerts the reader to the fact that a translator will be needed later.

Parentheses are also used in a number of ways in the same line as the character's name when a character is about to speak. These are used to convey a message to the director/producer using abbreviations to denote certain filmic terms:

(VO) Denotes that the character's voice is heard in a **voiceover** and is not seen speaking on screen for the duration of the speech.

(O/S) This means that the character speaking is **off screen** and is similar to the abbreviation above. However, the character could be just out of the frame of the film and their voice could still be heard off screen.

(Cont'd) or (CONT'D) This abbreviation stands for **continued** and is placed alongside the character's name when a character's speech continues in between action.

Here are a few examples, from *The Red Shoes*, of the above. Firstly, a **voiceover**:

Extract begins

```
EXT. STREET. EVENING.

The man looks down at Nothemba's feet through
the car window.

                    MAN
          Nice shoes ...

Nothemba screws her courage together and turns
towards him.

                    NOTHEMBA (VO)
          Left, right. It will all be alright.
```

Extract ends

Next, an example of **off screen** and a bonus **continued**:

Extract begins

```
                    PAUL
          Getting to his feet. He's really worried
          now)
          But you can't go out there at this time of
          night? It's not safe!

She puts her hand onto the handle.

                    PAUL (CONT'D)
          And you haven't got your car keys ...
          You ...
```

```
            (Trying a different tack)
        Shirley ... Please! I'm sorry!
        It'll never happen again ...

She is unmoved. She opens the door.

                    PAUL (CONT'D)
        You're coming back, aren't you?

She walks through the door without a backward glance.

                    PAUL
        Shirley!

She ignores him. Defeated for a moment, he
stares out after her as she walks out onto the
street with determination.

                    PAUL (VO) (CONT'D)
            (Almost to himself)
        You'll be back, Babe ... I know it ...

Shirley doesn't look back. Her bare feet seem to
sparkle under the streetlights.
```

Extract ends

Transitions

Cutting from one scene to the next is fairly straightforward. Final Draft provides a "transition" facility which allows one to click on "Cut To", "Fade Out", "Cross Fade", "Fade to Black" and so on. However, I recommend using these sparingly and only if you are completely sure of when to use these transitions. If you are not sure, it may be best to use the simpler: "Cut To".

There is a trend these days not to use any transition slug lines as producers say that it's obvious that the end of one scene leads to another. However, there is no hard and fast rule.

When you do use it, the transition slug line always hugs the right-hand margin of the script.

Here is another example from *The Red Shoes*:

Extract begins

INT. SUBURBAN LOUNGE - DUSK

SHIRLEY, a 30-something-year-old woman, is PACING up and down in the darkened lounge. She scrutinises the street outside the LACE CURTAINS as she passes the window. A frown creases her brow.

She turns towards the interior of the house. Pasting a false smile on her face, she walks towards the kitchen. LOUD MUSIC is blaring from the adjoining room.

CUT TO:

INT. SUBURBAN HOUSE KITCHEN - DUSK

A small RADIO is blaring dance music from the counter. The kitchen counter is a mess of leftover FOOD, PLATES, TOYS, general CHAOS. SCHOOL SHOES are scattered on the floor, and dirty CLOTHES lie piled up next to the WASHING MACHINE.

Three young CHILDREN are leaping around the table, dancing wildly to the music. The OLDER BOY, about eight years old, grabs his mother's hands as she walks into the kitchen. She goes straight towards the DISHES waiting to be washed in the SINK.

CROSS FADE TO:

INT. SHACK - DAWN (FLASHBACK)

Nothemba picks up one of her mother's SHOES from the floor. She holds the shiny red object and examines it closely.

Extract ends

Just for an extra dose of how to write a script well, here are the opening scenes from the powerful film *Joker* (2019) which went on to win a number of Oscars.

Extract begins

```
EXT. GOTHAM SQUARE, MIDTOWN - KENNY'S MUSIC
SHOP - DAY

GOTHAM SQUARE IS CLOGGED WITH TRAFFIC. Non-
stop honking horns, pedestrians crowding
the sidewalk. Huge billboards, giant movie
marquees, garbage bags piled high everywhere.
Underneath it all we hear a TINKLING PIANO
playing something bouncy and fast-paced.

FROM ACROSS THE BUSY CITY STREET, we see
Joker. He's dressed as a sad-faced HOBO CLOWN.
This is his job. Dressed in tattered clothes,
dark five o'clock shadow painted on his face,
big bulbous red nose, his mouth's outlined in
white, turned down at the corners.

He's holding up a sign in front of Kenny's
Music Shop that reads, "EVERYTHING MUST GO!"
A banner above the store reads, "GOING OUT OF
BUSINESS!"

Behind him, an OLD MAN plays a piano on the
street. Both of them there to draw attention
to the big sale going on in the store.

Joker's doing a little Charlie Chaplin like
waddle to the music. Most people walk right
past, ignoring him. A few bump into him by
mistake.

JOKER SEES A GROUP OF FIVE BOYS, no more than
15 years old, walking toward him. He moves out
of their way. They crack up laughing when they
see him. Start making fun of him.
```

Joker ignores them, tries to do his job the best he can while maintaining some dignity. Keeps dancing and holding up the sign.

One of the kids knocks the sign out of Joker's hands -

                    KID #1
          Suck my dick, clown.

The kids laugh. Joker doesn't say anything. Just bends over to pick up the sign -

Another kid kicks him in the ass -

                    KID #2
          Whoops.

Joker falls face first onto the sidewalk. Oddly, the old man playing the piano picks up the pace of the music - The kids crack up.

One of the boys grabs Joker's sign and takes off running across the street -

The other kids follow, weaving through traffic -

Joker gets up and gives chase. He needs his sign back. He almost gets hit by a taxi, spinning out of the way just in time - Spinning right into another taxi that stops just short of hitting him.

Joker keeps running through traffic. People stare. A clown barrelling down the street has got to be a joke -

EXT. CORNER, SIDE STREET - GOTHAM SQUARE - CONTINUOUS

The five boys are booking it down the crowded street laughing and whooping it up. At the last second they take a sharp right turn down a cross street –

Joker almost overshoots the corner, slip-sliding in his big red shoes – He rights himself and heads down after them – Sees them running up ahead –

WHAP! Out of nowhere Joker gets hit in the face!

He falls to the ground.

One of the kids was hiding between parked cars and hit Joker with the "EVERYTHING MUST GO!" sign, splintering it in two –

The other kids turn back and walk up to Joker down on the ground. Joker reaches out, still trying to save the sign –

THE KIDS START KICKING AND BEATING THE SHIT out of Joker. It's brutal and vicious. Nobody on the street stops to help.

CLOSE ON JOKER'S HOBO CLOWN FACE, down on the ground. Sweat running down his face, smearing his make-up. He doesn't even look like he's in pain. He just takes the beating. That stupid frown painted on his face.

Extract ends

Almost a Wrap

When you write your script you can use the extracts above as a guidelines. Refer to them whenever in doubt as to formatting any section of your script.

TASKS

1. Watch a number of your favourite films. Imagine what the script itself would look like while you are watching each film. How visual are these films? How much dialogue is used? Would you change anything if you could? Learn what you can from these films and put that into practice when you begin your last task.

2. Using all you have learnt in the past seven chapters and working from your detailed step outline, **Write Your Script!** Trust your instincts and use your inherent talent. There is no doubt that you have talent or you wouldn't have made it this far, completing the previous tasks successfully. Now write the best script you can.

Chapter 8

CROWDFUNDING

What is crowdfunding?

Is this the new way to make your movie? I wasn't too sure until I was lucky enough to encounter Peter Broderick in the Producers' Forum at the Durban Film Mart some years ago. I walked into his seminar where he was talking about the explosion of a new phenomenon at that time called crowdfunding (also called crowdsourcing). Peter Broderick is the president of Paradigm Consulting in the United States. His company helps filmmakers and media companies develop strategies to maximise distribution, improve audience reach, as well as increase revenues. He's been an advocate of the ultra-low-budget feature film movement for many years and is a passionate advocate of digital filmmaking.

I made extensive notes during his impressive presentation and the summation of the notes follows below.

A way to fund your film

As Broderick explained, crowdfunding is a concentric way to make money, but it is vital that you think of your AUDIENCE before you start your funding campaign. Remember that you have to do everything you can, use every marketing tool in the book, to create AWARENESS of your project. Broderick quoted some examples of how to do this:
- One producer incorporated a number of educational grants into his funding campaign so that the charity aspect of his drive could be emphasised and used to generate goodwill.
- Another successful group put their trailer online and invited people to remix it.
- A woman who wanted to fund her around-the-world yacht trip offered different rewards for certain amounts of money. If people donated $10, she promised them a Polaroid photo taken along her journey. $50 earned them a coconut sent from one of her destinations, and so on.

- Jennifer Fox, who crowdfunded her very personal project called *My Reincarnation,* sent personal thank-you letters to every single person who donated funds, from the smallest amounts of money to the largest sums.
- Some producers offered co-producer credits for a certain amount of Euros.

What is most important, however, is that the website you create to raise funds has to be FUN and encourage people to come back to the site. The more visitors you attract, the better your chances of raising funds. Don't fall into the trap of making your website nothing more than a press kit. Nothing is more boring than the unchanging dynamic of a press kit site. Broderick emphasised that it is imperative you keep the following elements in mind when creating your crowdfunding website:

- Fewer words, more PICTURES
- Rich VISUAL content relating to the movie
- Content must be constantly UPDATED – i.e., it must be dynamic
- Harness VIEWER'S INPUT in some way – people want to contribute
- Website must be PERSONAL and written in the first person
- A good VIDEO documenting the journey of the project is a must
- HUMOUR wins the day every time
- Use SOCIAL NETWORKING SITES to create awareness of your project.

The filmmaker must give actual information about the project on the site. Remember, piracy isn't your prime concern here, but obscurity is. Broderick showed a video example from a Spanish project that raised its funds through crowdfunding. The project was called *The Cosmonauts* and used humour and youthful energy to introduce the genesis of the film to the future audience. He also quoted an example of Neil Gaiman's *The Price* which used social networking sites, such as Twitter and Facebook, especially using the #BoingBoing hashtag to create awareness and to raise funds for production.

Broderick referred to a project created by self-confessed Finnish "nerds" who wanted to make a feature that was a spoof of *Star Trek*. They wrote a rough outline and put the draft online. This soon attracted a writer. They then asked for people to contribute special effects skills. In the end 3 000 people across 300 countries contributed to this project, which resulted in a 108-minute feature called *Star Wreck*. Thirty per cent of all the images contributed to the film were donated by people around the world who were happy just to be associated with the project. They all received screen credit. The project cost €23 000 in total. The makers of the film knew their audience. They appealed to a niche core audience of like-minded "nerds" such as themselves who would be delighted to contribute to a project they believed in. The final product is free to download but the makers of the film earned 20 times their original budget in revenue through DVD sales. Remarkably, even though everyone could download the film for nothing, people still wanted to own their own copies, especially if the film contained their names listed in the credits.

Another production that used crowdfunding successfully was an animation feature produced in Australia about global warming called *Coalition of the Willing* by Simon Robson. Twenty different companies produced different segments of the film, which was made in 30 different sections. Even though each section has a different style, the film fits together as a cohesive whole.

Broderick emphasised that the best way to get people to support a project is if they contribute to the making of the project in some way. It allows them to feel part of something as large as a film.

Broderick spoke at length about host websites such as www.kickstarter.com and www.IndieGoGo.com, both of which provide a platform to host crowd sourcing/funding projects. Both sites set dates for budget targets to be reached. Kickstarter takes a certain percentage of the income as payment, but IndieGoGo does so only if you don't make your target. Then they take nine per cent.

Advice for a successful crowdfunding website:
- Write the website in the first person to build awareness of the film
- Create a vision for the website that may be bigger than the film
- The website must take on a life of its own
- Make things you can sell that relate to your film
- Create some sort of payback for visitors, either through allowing them to download video streams or buy DVDs to related topics or even buy books on your site if they are of similar topics. (Broderick suggests you buy goods wholesale that you can sell retail on the website)

- Try to come up with giveaways or incentives to encourage donations
- Remember your objectives for the site are to build AWARENESS of the project and to RAISE MONEY. Keep this in mind at all times.

Broderick closed the seminar by referring to one of the first-ever cases of crowdfunding. The first *Oxford English Dictionary* was a literary example of crowdfunding. People came together from all walks of life to contribute words to this enormous literary work. It is almost certain that none of them was paid.

My Experience with Crowdfunding on IndieGoGo.com

After listening to Peter Broderick speaking about the many independent filmmakers who took a chance and launched their projects on one of the two best known crowdfunding websites in the USA, I decided that I'd have a go myself. After all, I had a slew of scripts producers hadn't wanted to make and I'd been working for nine years on a feature that carried my heart and soul. This particular feature was the film about my brother's suicide on the Angolan border during the apartheid border wars.

To remind you again, from the late 1960s, all white boys from the age of 16 onwards were conscripted into the South African Defence Force to do their military service. After three months of brutal basic training, they were deployed into various areas to quell the "unrest" of a population that had been oppressed too long.

My brother was drafted at the age of 17, when his dreams of becoming a rock star were just burgeoning. He was an artist, extremely sensitive and not made of the stuff that allows people to enjoy learning how to bayonet another human being to death. He broke out of the army during basics and stole a rifle to add to his horrendous act of going AWOL.

He returned home, and encouraged his fellow band members to take the rifle to a local rubbish dump, where they all took turns to fire rounds of bullets into the ash heap. Unbeknown to them, a homeless woman was sheltering in some part of the dump and she was killed by a ricochet bullet. They only found out about her death a few days later whenit was was reported in the newspaper. One of the members of my brother's band went to the police and told them that only Jimmy, my brother, had fired the rifle. By the time the police came to arrest him he'd already had a breakdown about the fact that he was responsible for the death of another human being.

Instead of putting him in prison, they sent him to a mental home. He was released some months later, a shadow of his former self. A few years passed and suddenly, after being classified as mentally unfit for military service after his breakdown, he was reclassified as fit and deployed to the front line of the border war. A friend who was there at the time said that Jimmy begged those in charge to let him serve in the kitchen rather than take up arms. Unfortunately, a brutal staff sergeant had it in for him and insisted he go into active combat. Three days after reaching the border he was dead. The official report said that he was killed by a ricochet bullet. However, his friend told me he'd taken his own life rather than go out to fight in a war he didn't believe in. Knowing my brother as I did, this version rang horribly true.

The reason it took so long to write this film is that I was heartbroken for many years.

Writing *A Shot at the Big Time*

It was 20 years before I could even contemplate writing my brother's story and then a further nine years before it became a good script. In the end I used composite characters and contracted the timeline to use all my skills to work to make this the best script it could be, based on the truth of my brother's desire to make music rather than war.

A number of producers optioned this script over the years. This meant that they'd "bought" the right to make this film for a minimal fee until we could raise the full budget. Unfortunately each one of the producers, including the ones who'd won South Africa's only Oscar, wanted to make changes so drastic that these would have affected the essence of the story. The way they wanted to film this script wouldn't have paid tribute to the sacrifice my brother had made. Each time I reached a point where I couldn't work with them and they released me from the agreement.

But that left me with a script in ninth draft, which had gone through many edits with two international script editors, who both thought it was one of the best stories they'd ever come across. So, alternatively, I tried to turn it into a novel but it was not too successful, as no-one wanted to publish it. And then I walked into Peter Broderick's seminar.

You know that feeling when you're suddenly aware that you're in the right place at the right time, that you couldn't be anywhere else more appropriate? That's the feeling I had when listening to Peter Broderick talk. Suddenly there was a way I could take this film into my own hands and ensure that I'd be able to make it the way I wanted to. I'd produced all my own plays and even directed a few over the past decade.

Raising a budget to make a play is so much more attainable than for a film. Especially as this film's budget wasn't small. This was, in part, a war movie, and it needed to be made extremely well to do it justice. It also included music, which would add to the cost.

Peter Broderick's seminar nestled at the back of my mind for a few months. In the middle of the chaos which is my daily life I harboured the thought that perhaps I should launch an IndieGoGo campaign on the 11th minute of the 11th day of the 11th month of 2011, this Remembrance Day was made more for being in 2011. I'd always remembered those who gave their lives for wars, willingly or unwillingly, on Remembrance Day, and this year it was a particularly special date. I made a few forays into IndieGoGo to see how it worked and it looked simple enough to set up a campaign. The only problem was that I didn't have any videos or promos filmed already to capture the public's interest.

Thank goodness for Jonathan Handley. His a friend who grew up in the same small town that I did and who knew my brother well. He'd been so inspired after reading my script that he'd written and recorded a number of songs especially for *A Shot at the Big Time*. Fortunately for me he'd also videoed two of the songs at his own expense and put them on YouTube. This was my way to launch the campaign with a bang.

On the morning of the 11th of the 11th 2011, I prepared to launch on IndieGoGo with Jonathan Handley's video of *Strum My Gun* and my synopsis of the film polished up as much as possible. In spite of launching this campaign by the seat of my pants, not too sure of what I was doing, I had an immediate and wonderful response. Friends from Australia donated first, and former scriptwriters I'd taught at the Wildlife Film Academy where I'd lectured for three years came forward. One of them, Paul Dwyer, donated the services of his visual graphics team in Australia to create a poster beyond anything I could've imagined. He also donated $1 000. A few larger donations came in from strangers and friends, but the campaign ran over Christmas and New Year. An incredible South African benefactor, Athol Williams, donated $1 000 and became very attached to the project. In the end I raised $5 260, which was not enough to make the feature film, but it garnered me public support, which outweighed any monetary value.

During the mere two months the campaign ran, I was offered the service of a website designer and editor who created a site specifically for *Shot*; a PR specialist, Sharlene Versveld, donated her time and effort to get me airtime on national radio stations as well as press coverage in national newspapers; a professional photographer, Val Adamson, offered to do the photoshoots on set; a retired head of an NGO donated her energy towards creating awareness among the End Conscription Campaign, which had tried to stop the enforced conscription during the 1980s; a member of the South African band *Freshlyground* offered to mix and record Jonathan Handley's original songs and compose the incidental music; three DOPs (directors of photography) offered their services to the film; an independent filmmaker offered us the use of his cameras and other film equipment; a university media school under the direction of Mike Hatton offered us the same – full use of their equipment and editing facilities as well as their students filming our electronic press kit. And, most importantly, I found the director: one of my former UKZN students and now practising filmmaker, Stephen de Villiers.

Then there were the online auditions. I decided to make use of an aspect of crowdfunding called Do It With Others – DIWO for short. Like the campaigns mentioned by Peter Broderick above, DIWO asks those who contribute to the film to make inputs into aspects of the some aspect of the filmmaking process. I decided to run online auditions for the main roles as well as for the music. The call for musicians was won hands-down by *Freshlyground*, as I mentioned above, but the auditions kept rolling in. It was fascinating to hear from people across the country desperate to have a role in this film, even when it seemed obvious that we weren't going to reach our target. I tried to encourage people to post their comments about each of the auditions ,but not many seemed keen to criticise their peers. In the end we found our lead actor for the critical role of Jimmy, Brad Backhouse. I know I couldn't have found anyone better through any other forum.

Using IndieGoGo as a funding platform allowed me to retain creative control of the project, because the director was someone I chose, someone I know well, and someone who respects my vision of the story as well as the rest of my work. This is usually an aspect of filmmaking that is removed from the control of the scriptwriter when a script is handed over to an anonymous director or producer. My experience on *White Lion* taught me that. It's especially important that the creative control remains with me on this particular project.

We completed the short film in 2012. It premiered at the Durban International Film Festival in 2013, which was a very proud moment for me and my family, who'd seen my efforts over the years. In 2014, *A Shot at the Big Time,* the short, was accepted into the Cannes Court Métrage (for short films), something that was beyond my wildest dreams. Thanks to one of the greatest benefactors on the planet, Athol Williams, I was able to travel to Cannes for the first time, and screen my short film there.

I recommend crowdfunding highly. Through crowdfunding you, as the writer and producer, retain creative control of your script, and your film finds an enormously wide audience depending on how well you use social networking sites.

I made use of IndieGoGo.com rather than Kickstarter.com as Kickstarter insists that you have a US bank account in which to deposit the funds in the end. IndieGoGo disburses the money into your own account in whatever country you are. It does take nine per cent and some change, for facilitating your project. I found IndieGoGo very user-friendly. They loved my DIWO campaign and made *Shot* their focus on their home page a number of times during the campaign. They were also very helpful when there was a hitch with the disbursement. They answered my queries promptly and sorted out a problem with my bank within days.

It was useful to have auditions to post every day or so, as it's vital to keep the website fresh and ticking over with new content. Constant updates about the progress of the project are also recommended to keep the donors informed about how their money will be used. It's also important to ensure you thank everyone who donates time or money or skill. I offered a co-producer credit for every $10 donated.

You can be as creative as you like with the rewards you give donors. It's fun to make the project as exciting as possible. When I started the campaign, my DIWO offered auditions not only for the acting roles but also for the poster and the music. The latter two were completed so successfully right at the beginning of the campaign that the other entrants were left standing. The acting auditions will continue for a few of the supporting roles right until the first frame is shot. The great thing about IndieGoGo is that the site remains live even though the funding campaign has stopped. You can continue to post updates and links to the site to keep it current, as we're doing with the final auditions.

I also suggest having a Facebook page or other website for your film to increase coverage of the film. The more visual the campaign is online, the better your chances of success. IndieGoGo gave me the launch-pad I needed and it has been an invaluable experience in taking the power into my own hands. When your script is strong enough, and **NOT** before then, take your chance to launch your film on one of these crowdfunding websites. South Africa has its own equivalents now: Thundafund and GoFundMe, so take a look at those too. I wish you only luck and all good things with your film's journey.

References

http://www.peterbroderick.com/bio/bio.html
http://coalitionfilm.blogspot.com/
http://www.wreckamovie.com/
http://www.kickstarter.com/
http://www.indiegogo.com/
Link to *A Shot at the Big Time* electronic press kit is on www.janetvaneeden.com

CONCLUSION

FEEDBACK

Writing is something that everyone does to a greater or lesser degree, thanks to general education systems. Everyone is able to write at least a letter or a short essay.

Unfortunately, the fact that everyone is able to write allows people to think that they are writers too. If only they had enough time or weren't committed to another profession, they too would write a novel and a film, as I've been told many times.

The irrefutable fact of the matter is, however, that writers are people who write whenever and wherever they can. The dedication and commitment required to write a sustained piece of work, whether it's a film script or a novel, is frequently underestimated. So, it is with a word of caution that I advise you to take the next step as you put your work out into the world.

Now that you have written your script, you will be desperate to get feedback from a reliable source. Firstly, give your script to a few trusted friends. They may be kind and give you positive feedback only. In my experience, though, everyone's a critic, and they want to prove that they are better than you. It is sometimes a shock to hear your best friend rip your script apart and tell you how you should have written it. However, you may be lucky enough to have more considerate friends. Hopefully they will tell you gently where you could improve your script. If you are really lucky there may be a few people around you who will be qualified enough to give you constructive advice.

Try not to be too wounded by the criticism people level at you. Take whatever is useful from their comments and use whatever advice resonates with your vision of the script. Try not to take their criticisms too personally. Very often people who haven't written their own stories take their frustrations out on your script. I have found that the best people to critique your work are those who have written their own scripts or novels and don't need to rewrite your script to assuage their thwarted aspirations.

Once you are happy enough with your work to send your script out into the professional world, you may/should engage a script editor to give your work professional feedback. A good script editor is invaluable. Remember my warning above to use script editors who write themselves. There is nothing more dangerous than a script editor who resents you for achieving what they haven't been able to achieve.

Contact the various writers' organisations in your area. The Writers' Guild in Britain, the Screenwriters Guild in the United States, and the Writers' Guild of South Africa are extremely useful bodies. In the US and Britain, it is mandatory to become a member of these Guilds. The Writers' Guild of South Africa is working towards such a mandate too. These groups will be able to put you in touch with other writers and script editors and give insight into the industry in your country.

It is essential that you join as many professional writing bodies and film organisations as possible. Websites have a huge role to play in helping you on your path. The website I used the most was a British one called TwelvePoint.com. South Africa has its own FilmContact.com and ScreenAfrica.com, which provide access to filmmakers in this country.

It's vital to build a network of contacts who understand what you do. The average person in the street doesn't have a clue about screenwriting, and you may find yourself disheartened if you don't have a support group.

Look online to find the contact details of writers' guilds, National Film and Video Foundation, the National Arts Council, the KwaZulu-Natal Film Commission and other useful writing bodies and websites.

If you are lucky enough to know someone who works in the industry, as I was, ask them to read your script before anyone else. In my experience, one professional friend is worth a million acquaintances who think they know what they are talking about.

People like Richard E Grant and Ian Roberts, one of South Africa's veteran actor/writer/directors, who read my screenplays as I wrote them, had the inside knowledge of the industry, and gave me the belief in myself to continue on this difficult path.

Finally, writing for films is not easy. Because of the budgets involved in making a feature film, even with the more democratic HD digital options these days, it may take years before your feature hits the big screen.

However, if you believe in yourself and your film strongly enough, persevere. This is the single attribute that separates the real film writers from the wannabes. That and exceptional talent, obviously.

A simple maxim I read when I first started writing all those years ago has stayed with me. It has kept me going through many, many disappointments. It may be trite, but a cliché is a cliché only because it's true. It was a sentence I read in a writing magazine and it resonated with me deeply. It said:

The only people who succeed are those who don't give up.

Do not give up. Believe in yourself and your script and you will get there in the end.

I wish you the very best of luck on this most difficult, but eternally fascinating, path of scriptwriting.

Contact details

KZN Film Commission: https://kznfilm.co.za/
National Film and Video Foundation: htttps://www.nfvf.co.za/
Indiegogo: https://www.indiegogo.com/

REFERENCES

12 Years a Slave. [DVD] 2013. Steve McQueen. UK. Regency Enterprises.
Abel, E, Hirsch, M, & Langland, E. 1983. *The Voyage In: Fictions of Development*. Hanover: University Press of New England.
Abel, E. 1983. "Narrative Structure(s) and Development." In *The Voyage In: Fictions of Development*. Hanover: University Press of New England.
Adaptation, 2002. [DVD] Spike Jonze. USA. Sony Pictures.
Alexander, M. 1989. *Women in Romanticism: Mary Wollstonecraft, Dorothy Wordsworth and Mary Shelley*. Basingstoke, Hants: Macmillan.
Altman, R. 1984. "A Semantic/Syntactic Approach to Film Genre." *Cinema Journal*, Vol. 23, no. 3 (Spring 1984) pp. 6–18. University of Texas Press on behalf of the Society for Cinema & Media Studies. http://www.jstor.org/stable/1225093 (Accessed 6 October 2015)
Aristotle. 1961. *Aristotle's Poetics: Translation and Analysis*. New York: Straus and Giroux.
Aronson, L. 2001. *Screenwriting Updated*. New York: Silman-James Press.
Aronson, L. 2010. *The 21st Century Screenplay: A Comprehensive Guide to Writing Tomorrow's Films*. London: Allen & Unwin.
Arrival. [DVD] 2016. Denis Villeneuve. USA. Paramount Pictures.
A Shot at the Big Time, the Short. [DVD] 2013. Stephen de Villiers. SA. Shot Productions.
Ballard, N, Daley, K & Hahn, S. 2014. *The Heroine's Journey Project*. https://heroinejourneys.com/heroines-journey/comment-page-1/#comment-86 (Accessed 16 November 2016)
Barnsley, MF & Rising, H. 1993. *Fractals Everywhere*, 2nd ed. Boston, MA: Academic Press.
Barr, T. 2012. *Fangirl: The Heroine's Journey: Defining Concepts* http://fangirlblog.com/2012/04/the-heroines-journey-how-campbells-model-doesnt-fit/ (Accessed 11 April 2016)
Beilin, EV. 1987. *Women Writers of the English Renaissance*. Princeton: Princeton University Press.
Being John Malkovich. [DVD] 1999. Spike Jonze. USA. Astralwerks.
Bingham, D. 2010. *Whose Lives Are They Anyway? The Biopic as Contemporary Film Genre*. New Jersey: Rutgers University Press.
Bonnet, J. 2006. *Stealing Fire from the Gods*. California: Michael Wiese Productions.
Booker, C. 2006. *The Seven Basic Plots: Why We Tell Stories*. London, New York: Continuum International Publishing Group.
Bordwell, D. 2008. *Poetics of Cinema*. New York and London: Routledge.
Bordwell, D & Thompson, K. 2008. *Film Art – An Introduction*. 8th ed. University of Wisconsin: MacGraw-Hill.
Brant, C & Purkiss, D, eds. 1992. *Women, Texts and Histories, 1575–1760*. London: Routledge.

Campbell, J. 1949. *The Hero with a Thousand Faces.* New York: Penguin.
Campbell, J. 2013. *Goddesses.* California: New World Library.
Canonici, NN. 1986. *Izinganekwam – An Anthology of Zulu Folktales.* Durban: University of Natal.
Canonici, CC. 1995. "Folktale performance as an educational experience." *Southern African Journal for Folktale Studies,* Vol. 6, pp. 13–23.
Canonici, NN. 1990. *The Zulu Folktale.* Durban: University of Natal.
Conway, JK. 1999. *When Memory Speaks: Exploring the Art of Autobiography.* New York, Vintage Books.
Coombe, RJ. 1993. "The Properties of Nature and the Politics of Possessing Identity: Nature Claims in Cultural Appropriation." *Canadian Journal of Law and Jurisprudence.* Vol. VI. no. 2. (July 1993).
Cunningham, K. 2008. *Soul of Screenwriting: 16 Story Steps: On Writing, Dramatic Truth, and Knowing Yourself.* London, New York: Continuum International Publishing Group.
Dällenbach, L. 1977. *Le Récit Spéculaire: Essai Sur la Mise en Abyme.* Paris: Seuil.
Dancyger, K & Rush, J. 2007. *Alternative Scriptwriting: Successfully Breaking the Rules.* Amsterdam: Elsevier.
Dankert, SC ed. 1992. *The Quotable Johnson: A Topical Compilation.* San Francisco: Ignatius Press.
De Nooy, J. 1991. "The Double Scission: Dällenbach, Doležel, and Derrida on Doubles." *Style* Vol. 25, no. 1, pp. 19–27.
Dick, BF. 1998. *Anatomy of Film,* 3rd ed. New York: St Martin's Press.
Dlamini, KH. 2012. Home video of Umhlonyana.
Egri, L. 1972. *The Art of Dramatic Writing.* New York: Simon & Schuster Adult Publishing Group.
Erin Brockovich. [DVD] 2000. Stephen Soderbergh. USA. Universal Pictures.
Ferguson, M. 1993. *Colonialism and Gender Relation from Mary Wollstonecraft to Jamaica Kincaid: East Caribbean Connections.* New York: Colombia University Press.
Field, S. 1984. *The Screenwriter's Workbook.* New York: Dell.
Field, S. 2005. *Screenplay: The Foundations of Screenwriting.* New York: Bantam.
Foreman, Milos. 1975. *One Flew Over the Cuckoo's Nest.* USA, California: United Artists.
Fremgen, J. 1998. "The Magicality of the Hyena." *Asian Folklore Studies,* Vol. 57, pp. 331–344.
Friedman, J. 2000. *How to Make Money Scriptwriting.* Exeter: Intellect Books.
Genette, G. 1980. *Narrative Discourse.* Translated by Jane Lewin. Ithaca: Cornell University Press.
Gilbert, S & Gubar, S. 2000. *The Madwoman in the Attic: The Woman Writer and the Nineteenth Century Literary Imagination.* Yale: Yale University Press.

Godwin, W, Clemit, P & Walker, GL. Eds. 2001. *Memoirs of the Author of A Vindication of the Rights of Woman*. Peterborough: Broadview Press.

Goldman, W. 1989. *Adventures in the Screen Trade*. New York: Grand Central Publishing.

Gordon, C. 2015. *Romantic Outlaws: The Extraordinary Lives of Mary Wollstonecraft and Mary Shelley*. London: Random House.

Gordon, L. 2005. *Mary Wollstonecraft, A New Genus*. London: Little, Brown.

Gordon, L. 2014. *Divided Lives – Dreams of a Mother and Daughter*. London, Virago.

Grant, C & Kuhn, A. Eds. 2006. *Screening World Cinema: A Screen Reader*. London: Routledge.

Grant, RE. 2006. *The Wah-Wah Diaries: The Making of a Film*. London: MacMillan.

Graour, K. 2014. *The Four Degrees of Narrative Separation: Exploring the Process of Narrative Adaptation through Biographical Texts*. University of Cape Town MA thesis.

Griggs, LS. 2012. *Hero Quest Cycle Explained*. https://questcycles.com/hero-quest (Accessed 16 November 2016)

hooks, b. 1990. *Yearning: Race, Gender and Cultural Politics*. Toronto: Between the Lines Press.

Internet Movie Data Base. *Most Popular Biography Feature Films*. http://www.imdb.com/search/title?genres=biography&title_type=feature&sort=moviemeter,asc (Accessed: 4 January 2015)

Into the Wild. [DVD] 2007. Sean Penn. USA. Paramount Pictures.

Invictus. [DVD] 2009. Clint Eastwood. USA. Warner Brothers.

Jaide, D. 2009. *Oshun The African Goddess of Beauty, Love, Prosperity, Order and Fertility*. Africa House Articles. http://www.africaresource.com/rasta/sesostris-the-great-the-egyptian-hercules/oshun-the-african-goddess-of-beauty-love-prosperity-order-and-fertility/ (Accessed 24 October 2016)

Jefferson, A. 1983. "'Mise en Abyme' and the Prophetic in Narrative." *Style*, Vol. 17, no. 2, pp. 196–208.

Jones, V. 2000. *Women and Literature in Britain, 1700–1800*. Cambridge: Cambridge University Press.

Joubert, E. 1978. *Die Swerfjare van Poppie Nongena*. Cape Town: Tafelberg.

Jung, CG. 1969. *Archetypes and the Collective Unconscious*, Collected Works of CG Jung, Volume 9 (Part 1), Princeton: Princeton University Press.

Kaplan, C. 1986. *Sea Changes: Culture and Feminism*. London: Verso.

Katz, E, Blumler, JG, & Gurevitch, M. 1973. "Uses and Gratifications Research." *The Public Opinion Quarterly*, Vol. 34, no. 4, pp. 509–523.

Kelly, G. 1993. *Women, Writing and Revolution – 1790–1827*. Oxford: Clarendon Press.

Khumalo, ZLM. 1995. "The Portrayal of Themes in Blose's Uqomisa Mina Nje Uqomisa Iliba." University of Zululand MA thesis.

Lane, M. 1989. *Literary Daughters*. London: Robert Hale.

Langland, E. 1993. "Stories of Experience." *The Voyage In: Fictions of Development*. Hanover: University Press of New England.

Lawlor, PM. 1985. "Lautréamont, Modernism, and the Function of Mise en Abyme." *The French Review*, Vol. 58, no. 6, pp. 827–834.

Long Walk to Freedom. [DVD] 2013. Justin Chadwick. SA. VideoVision Entertainment.

Macris, A. 2004. "Samuel Beckett, Claude Simon and the 'Mise en abyme' of paradoxical duplication." *Samuel Beckett Today/Aujourd'Hui*, Vol. 14, pp. 117–129.

Makhubane Tshabalala, N. 2016. *Chronicles of Tshabalala Clan in Mhlongamuula and Its Exodus*. Wandsbeck, South Africa: Reach Publications.

Mandelbrot, B. 1983. *The Fractal Geometry of Nature*. San Francisco: WH Freeman.

Marcel, K & Smith, S. 2013. *Saving Mr Banks*. Screenplay. Los Angeles: Walt Disney Company.

Marggraff, M. 1994. The Moral Theme in Zulu Literature: A Progression (1930–1955). University of Pretoria MA dissertation.

Marggraff, M. 1998. "The Moral Theme in Zulu Literature: A Progression". *Literator*, Vol. no. 19 pp. 93–107. Pretoria: University of Pretoria.

Mendes, Sam, (1999) *American Beauty*. USA, California: Dreamworks Productions.

McKee, R. 1998. *Story: Substance, Structure, Style and the Principles of Screenwriting*. London: Methuen.

Michel, AP. 2008. "An Image Mise en Abyme." *Technology and Culture*, Vol. 49, no. 4, pp. 967–973.

Msimang, CT. 1991. *Inkosi Yinkosi Ngabantu*. Pretoria: Out of Africa Publishers.

Murdock, M. 1990. *The Heroine's Journey*. Boulder, Colorado: Shambala Publications, Inc.

Phoswa, FM. 2015. Home videos of the *Umhlonyane* ceremony.

Phoswa, FM. 2016. Interviews with Janet van Eeden.

Poovey, M. 1984. *The Proper Lady and the Woman Writer: Ideology as Style in the Works of Mary Wollstonecraft, Mary Shelley and Jane Austen*. Chicago: University of Chicago Press.

Roberts, AF. 1995. *Animals in African Art: From the Familiar to the Marvelous*. New York: Museum of African Art, Prestel.

Rogers, RA. 2006. "From Cultural Exchange to Transculturation: A Review and Reconceptualization of Cultural Appropriation." *Communication Theory: International Communication Association*, Vol. 6, pp. 274–503.

Saving Mr Banks. [DVD] 2013. John Lee Hancock. UK. Walt Disney Pictures.

Scafadi, S. 2005. *Who Owns Culture?: Appropriation and Authenticity in American Law.* London: Rutgers University Press.

Seger, L. 2003. *Advanced Screenwriting*, Los Angeles: Silman-James Press.

Selma. [DVD] 2014. Ava DuVernay. USA. Cloud Eight Films.

Shainberg, Stephen, (2006). *Fur: An Imaginary Portrait of Diane Arbus.* Pressman Film, Santa Monica, California, USA.

Snow, M. 2016. "Into the Abyss: a study of the mise en abyme." London Metropolitan University PhD thesis.

Stato, J. 1991. "Cultural Appropriation." *Off Our Backs*, Vol. 21, no. 9 (October 1991).

Steyn, M. 2001. *Whiteness Just Isn't What It Used to Be: White Identity in a Changing South Africa.* New York. State University of New York Press.

Synecdoche, New York. [DVD] 2008. Charlie Kaufman. USA. Sidney Kimmel Entertainment.

The Eternal Sunshine of the Spotless Mind. [DVD] 2004. Stephen Gondry. USA. Focus Features.

Todd, J. 1993. *Mary Wollstonecraft and the Rights of Death. Gender, Art and Death.* Cambridge: Polity Press.

Tomalin, C. 1992. *The Life and Death of Mary Wollstonecraft.* Rev. ed. New York: Penguin.

Van Eeden, J. 2001. *A Savage from the Colonies* (produced stage play).

Van Eeden, J. 2002. *A Savage Civilian* (produced stage play).

Van Eeden, J. 2010. *A Shot at the Big Time* (the feature script).

Van Eeden, J. 2012. *A Shot at the Big Time* (the short script).

Van Eeden, J. 2011. *Cut to the Chase: Scriptwriting for Beginners.* Johannesburg: Espresso Books.

Van Eeden, J. 2004. *The Savage Sisters* (produced stage play).

Vogler, C. 1996. *Writer's Journey: Mythic Structure for Storytellers and Screenwriters.* London: Boxtree.

White Lion. [DVD] 2010. Michael Swan. SA. Peru Pictures.

Wollstonecraft, M. 1792. *A Vindication of the Rights of Woman with Strictures on Moral and Political Subjects.* London: Joseph Johnson.

Wollstonecraft, M. 1787. *Thoughts on the Education of Daughters: With Reflections on Conduct, in the More Important Duties of Life.* London: Joseph Johnson.

Wollstonecraft, M. 1790. *A Vindication of the Rights of Men, in a Letter to the Right Honourable Edmund Burke.* London: Joseph Johnson.

Wollstonecraft, M. 1794. *An Historical and Moral View of the French Revolution; and the Effect it has Produced in Europe.* London: Joseph Johnson.

Acknowledgements

How do you begin to thank anyone for a lifetime's work in a particular field? I think I'll start at home, because if it weren't for their support, I wouldn't have been able to follow my dreams. Firstly, thanks are definitely due to my late parents, Helen and Hugh Openshaw, for their unending love and faith in me. Then to my husband, Richard Harrison, who has always stood by and supported me, even when he wasn't too sure what I was up to. Thanks to my three most-beloved children, James, William and Caitlin, who've always been so proud of everything I've done and are definitely my reason for being.

Muses along the way have definitely been Richard E Grant, Ian Roberts and most lately, Richard Green and Marina Bekker who recognised my talent as a writer and continue to motivate me.

Thanks to Julian Friedmann, my long-suffering agent, who thought my writing wasn't too shabby way back in 2001.

I'd also like to thank all the students I've taught through these many years, and fellow writers I've worked with, in this country and others. I've learnt so much from you and each encounter brought me fresh insights.

Thanks to the first editor of this manuscript, Margot Bertlesmann Doherty, whose enthusiastic reception gave me hope. Thanks also to Andy Thesen who did the book layout. And lastly, thanks to Colleen Higgs for believing in this project enough to take it on, and for finally bringing it to birth. I am grateful to you all.

About the author

Janet van Eeden started writing plays and screenplays over 26 years ago. Six of her plays went to the National Arts Festival in Grahamstown in the early 2000s, all funded by the National Arts Council. Her first screenplay to reach the screen was *White Lion* in 2010. She wrote and produced the short film, *A Shot at the Big Time*, which screened at the Cannes Short Film Metrage in 2014. She did her Masters and her PhD in English "by mistake", and received Cum Laude for the first and a lovely red robe for the second. She script-edits and evaluates many feature films for the KZN Film Commission, amongst others. She is the Overall Chairperson of both the Simon Sabela Awards as well as the SAFTAs. Janet is currently the Dean of AFDA Durban.

Janet van Eeden doesn't just teach screenwriting ... she IS screenwriting! She is able to bring invaluable first-hand experience to her online course, including many personal examples from her own work. If it hadn't been for Janet I would not have been able to complete my screenplay, a realisation of a long-held ambition and an accomplishment of which I'm very proud. – Julian Desser, journalist and copywriter, UK

Janet read two of my scripts: her feedback was intelligent, constructive and, most important to me, respected the intent of the work. She showed uncanny ability to get inside of the story and suggest subtle improvements to both character and structure. I could not imagine a more skilful teacher for the art of screenwriting. – Mark Lyon, editor-in-chief, *Cargovision Magazine*, USA

Janet's online screenwriting course was fun as well as highly instructive. I highly recommend the course not only for beginners but also as an important refresher for the more advanced screenwriter. – Gordon Slack, aeronautical engineer, UK

www.ingramcontent.com/pod-product-compliance
Lightning Source LLC
Chambersburg PA
CBHW020411230426
43664CB00009B/1256